Chapel Arm

Chapel Arm

Step Taylor

Chapel Arm
first published 2009 by
Scirocco Drama
An imprint of J. Gordon Shillingford Publishing Inc.

Scirocco Drama Editor: Glenda MacFarlane
Cover design by Terry Gallagher/Doowah Design Inc.
Author photo by Stephen Moss
Printed and bound in Canada on 100% post-consumer recycled paper.

We acknowledge the financial support of the Manitoba Arts Council, The Canada Council for the Arts and the Government of Canada through the Book Publishing Industry Development Program (BPIDP) for our publishing program.

Production inquiries should be addressed to:
tayloration_x@hotmail.com

Library and Archives Canada Cataloguing in Publication

Taylor, Step, 1985-
Chapel Arm / Step Taylor.

A play.
ISBN 978-1-897289-44-0

I. Title.

PS8639.A966C43 2009 C812′.6 C2009-904264-9

J. Gordon Shillingford Publishing
P.O. Box 86, RPO Corydon Avenue, Winnipeg, MB Canada R3M 3S3

Acknowledgements

Thanks to the Vagabond Trust—the writers' group to which I will always belong and from which I will always want feedback, siblings Christopher, Emily and Charlie, parents Stephen, Doreen, Harriet and Bob, classmates and instructors at the University of British Columbia, Ilkay Silk and Theatre St. Thomas, the NotaBle Acts Summer Theatre Festival, and most of my ex-girlfriends. *Chapel Arm* is dedicated to the town's real life inhabitants.

Step Taylor

Step Taylor is a twenty-four-year-old playwright, poet and novice screenwriter currently enrolled in the University of British Columbia's Optional Residency Creative Writing MFA Program. Taylor spent his childhood in the titular village of Chapel Arm, Newfoundland but has been based out of Fredericton, New Brunswick, since 1999.

During his undergraduate work at St. Thomas University, Taylor began acting in and writing for the Black Box Theatre. His original one-acts *Ask Kathy Who's Pathetic* (2005), *Weird and Picky* (2006) and *I Unclick* (2007) received readings at the annual "78" public workshop. Taylor won the NotaBle Acts Summer Theatre Festival's "Taking it to the Street" Playwriting Contest on three consecutive occasions with *The Father and Floozy Fiasco* (2004), *Shoes That Aren't Red* (2005) and *Stop My Vitals* (2006), all receiving performances. *Chapel Arm* was also staged by the company in the Black Box Theatre, August 2008.

Step is currently developing a new play, *Fuzzy Waters*, the story of a cell phone sales consultant who considers becoming a serial killer.

Characters

BEV

JAMIE

DOREEN

ART

Production History

Chapel Arm premiered at Black Box Theatre as the main stage show for NotaBle Acts Summer Theatre Festival, Fredericton, NB, on July 22, 2008, with the following cast:

JAMIE .... Greg Gale
DOREEN .... Marissa Allison
BEV ....Leah Holder
ART .... Robbie O'Neill

Directed by Rose Plotek
Stage managed by Jennifer April Butler
Sound design and original music by Michael Doherty
Lighting design by Chris Saad
Set design by Nicholas Cole

Act I

Scene 1

It's Wednesday at 12:14 AM. Chapel Arm, Newfoundland. A dank basement with unnecessary rugs that are even more unnecessarily filthy. An elderly couch of stains, rips, creases and faded flowers mopes in front of a generously nicked bar. The bar, rarely touched by genuinely functional adults, has some fearsome poker hands taped to it, as well as a lady poster or two from the informative pages of Maxim. *An old hunting license might be on display, and certainly there's a portrait of a limp bull moose. There's probably a broken Big Mouth Billy Bass loitering at the bar. BEV, a 30-year-old beautician, lies on the couch, thankfully separated from its withered skin by a quilt in narrowly better condition; she nonchalantly knits a multicoloured scarf that Dennis Rodman might have dropped a few grand on in his heyday. She sees a pack of Canadian Classics cigarettes on a nearby table and swipes them. She goes as far as sliding a cigarette into her palm, but silent assessment kills the natural chain of smoky events, and she tucks the cigarette in with the rest of its brothers and sisters. JAMIE, 28, spent and humming, walks through the basement door in his favourite gray T-shirt and some grass stained, soil browned blue jeans that have called his lower body home for the better part of a week. He carries a bag of work clothes. Coinciding with JAMIE's entrance is BEV's hiding of the pack of cigarettes beneath her unsightly, unshapely quilt. JAMIE's humming is reserved and privately pleasurable.*

BEV: Twelve t'irty at night, jus' so yuh knows.

JAMIE: I knows, b'y.

BEV: Pretty late time uh night tuh be gettin' home to yer woman.

JAMIE: Yuh don't say.

JAMIE returns to humming as he tosses the bag of clothes somewhere suitable and hurls his shoes towards the door.

BEV: Yuh could uh jus' took 'em off when yuh come in deh door, hey b'y.

JAMIE just hums, hums, hums.

What's d'at racket yer at?

JAMIE: Yuh knows it, girl.

JAMIE slows down the humdinger to what he perceives to be a BEV-able tempo.

BEV: Sounds right familiar, like.

JAMIE takes a serious breath, then starts in again at what he predicts will be the most recognizable verse.

Oh yes b'y! I knows d'at! (*Underscored by JAMIE's dead-on humming.*) We are chil'ren, chil'ren uh deh light. We is (*Some hesitation.*) shiny—in deh dark an' in deh light—

JAMIE: Go on, b'y. It's we are *shining* in deh darkness uh deh night.

BEV: How'm I supposed tuh remember d'at ol' t'ing, yuh fool?

JAMIE: Couldn't ever forget "Chil'ren uh deh Light," me ducky.

BEV: Children uh me arse.

JAMIE: (*To himself.*) Where'd I put me smokes to—

BEV: Yuh had a phone call, by deh way.

JAMIE looks about the room.

JAMIE: Right on.

BEV: Why yuh started on d'at song fur?

JAMIE fingers his pockets, retrieving only an empty pack of cigarettes.

JAMIE: Dunno b'y.

JAMIE walks about the room, scanning.

BEV: I never liked d'at as deh school song. Too churchy, hey b'y.

JAMIE: Uh school called Holy Trinity Sacred Heart Element'ry is always gonna have a churchy song, Bev.

BEV: "Chil'ren uh deh Light" d'ough? Sounds creepy, sure.

JAMIE: Says deh creepiest woman I ever known. (*Beat.*) Where deh fuck's me cig'rettes to?

BEV: Dunno b'y. (*Beat.*) I don't t'ink I ever knew all deh words to it.

JAMIE: Dare say yuh didn't, missus.

BEV: I had supper wit' Sharon and Jamie Sr. tonight—

JAMIE: I knows I left me extra pack here d'is afternoon. Fuck, I needs a cig'rette.

BEV: Yuh don't *needs* one.

JAMIE: Mind now.

BEV: Yuh don't needs it, b'y…do yuh?

JAMIE: Wha'?

BEV: Nudding.

JAMIE: Where is me cig'rettes to, Bev?

BEV: Got no clue, mah son.

JAMIE: Tell deh trut'.

BEV: Jamie, b'y— I wouldn't tell uh word of uh a lie to yuh, me love.

JAMIE: Whur d'ey to d'en?

BEV: Jamie, I—

JAMIE lifts up the scarf to reveal his hidden smokes.

(*Quietly.*) D'ere d'ey is.

JAMIE: By deh Geeeeezus.

BEV: Shouldn't be at it.

JAMIE: (*Lighting the cigarette and puffing heavily.*) Oh I knows.

BEV: Kills uh t'ousand brain cells before yur 'alfway t'rough one.

JAMIE: No it don't, yuh stupid arse. It hurts yer lungs.

BEV: Yuh, but yuh gets stupider every time yuh decides tuh take uh puff.

JAMIE: (*Savoring each interaction with the stick and smiling widely.)* Oh yuh. I 'ates it so much.

BEV: Anyway, *loser*, I 'ad supper wit' yer mudder and fodder.

JAMIE: Yuh, yuh said, yuh cig'rette burg'lar you.

BEV: D'ere's t'ree or faur moose steaks still up in deh fridge. Bowl uh potato salad too.

JAMIE: Dudn't matter. You say dur was uh call fur me?

BEV: Deadly feed. D'ey just went out to deh cabin fur deh week not too long 'go.

JAMIE: Yuh.

BEV: Yer dad saved some of he's holidays up so he could take uh long weekend now.

JAMIE: Must be nice. Who phoned fur me?

BEV: Luh, I knows yuh 'ates 'em right now, but—

JAMIE: Bev, all I wants tuh know—

BEV: Well, Jamie b'y, yuh is almost t'irty and living out uh he's basement. It's time yuh moves out town to me apartment. Or we could get a bigger place now deh once.

JAMIE: Whattaya goin' on wit'? I'm not t'irty. I'll be twenty-nine next week. Not d'at Fodder would know. Mind now. Me goin' out d'ere wit' deh townie crooks an' wiggers.

BEV: Jamie, yuh don't have tuh be right prickish about it.

JAMIE: Jumpin' Joseph Jesus FUCK! Who was on deh god blessed phone?

BEV: Can't we finish what we wus talkin' about first?

JAMIE: We are, b'y. I was just hummin' along, mindin' me business. D'en you starts up like uh hen wit' uh egg caught in yer arse.

BEV: Oh mah Jesus, Jamie.

JAMIE: Well.

BEV: Yuh drives me nuts sometimes.

JAMIE: Yeeees b'y. Feelin' is right mutual, hey.

BEV: Yuh never even takes deh idea serious. Yuh poisons me, Jamie.

JAMIE: Oh yuh.

BEV: Just come out town. Yuh could go to deh clubs more, hey b'y.

JAMIE: Last time I went down deh club wit' you we ended up takin' anodder missus back to yer place.

BEV: And yer complainin'.

JAMIE: I'm jus' sayin'—I couldn't be at d'at every weekend. Have deh bird beat right off me, hey b'y.

BEV: Well, we wouldn't be at it every weekend.

JAMIE: Becomes a dirt bag pretty quick bein' at d'at.

BEV: Yuh needs tuh move, mah son.

JAMIE: I'm nah movin', Bev, so yuh can screw off about it.

BEV: Fine d'en. (*Beat.*) I only told 'er tuh come back 'cause I t'ought yuh'd like it.

BEV returns to knitting, obviously dejected. JAMIE tosses his bag to the floor and sits next to her.

JAMIE: I knows d'at. I 'ad fun. (*Beat.*) I didn't mean tuh snap atcha.

BEV: Whatever.

JAMIE: I loves yuh.

BEV: (*Dismissively, knitting.*) Yes b'y.

JAMIE: I loves yuh tuh deat'.

BEV: I knows.

JAMIE throws his arms over her, reeling her into a hug.

Yuh stinks.

She feebly fights the hug. He persists.

JAMIE: I don't smell nudding.

BEV: Yuh stinks uh fish, yuh sonuvabitch.

JAMIE: I works at uh fish plant, Bev. I ain't coming home smellin' like yer mudder's forget-me-nots er nudding.

BEV: Yuh stinks right bad, like.

JAMIE: But I loves yuh some lot.

BEV: I loves you too, b'y, but I don't loves capelin—

JAMIE: Whattaya drinkin' tonight, missus?

BEV: Nah drinkin' a'tall.

JAMIE: I means what can I getcha.

BEV: Don't need nudding. Gotta drive out town ear'ly tamarrow.

JAMIE: Yuh works some hard, girl. Lemme fix yuh some'tin'.

BEV: Yuh gots neid'er cooler?

JAMIE: N'are one.

BEV: Malibu?

JAMIE: D'is is me 'ouse. Not no gay bar.

BEV: Well lard t'underin'.

JAMIE: I got Black 'Orse and Cap'in Morgan. And d'at's it.

BEV: Disgustin', mah son.

JAMIE: Morgan and he's steed.

BEV: I'll take uh beer, I s'ppose.

JAMIE: Datta girl.

He pats her leg and moves for the bar. He grabs a beer and starts fixing a rum and coke for himself.

So Bev—

BEV: Wha'?

JAMIE: *Who in deh bejesus called fur me?*

BEV: Oh yeeeeah.

JAMIE: *(A parrot.)* Oh yeeeeahhh.

BEV: Art Pretty called fur yuh, man.

JAMIE: Go on wit'cha.

BEV: He did too. I was 'alf tempted to call deh police on d'at geezer. What nerve he got getting me on the phone after burnin' down he's poor sister's property like d'at last mont'.

JAMIE: Whoa now. Yuh knows fine well he's "poor sister" left town after deh man was so frigged up—

BEV: What odds, b'y. She gives 'em uh 'ouse tuh live in for all d'ose years. Dudn't matter if she just wanted tuh get deh fuck outta Chapel Arm. Pro'lly deh reason she left was 'cause 'er brudder went right retarded-like when he's wife died. Yuh cries when somebody is dead…yuh don't just start t'rowin' gas'line and matches on 'ouses an' making smores or whatever deh fuck dey's called. Yuh cremates bodies, not 'ouses. An' really now… two 'ouses in a little more d'an ten years? D'at's not fit d'at ain't, b'y. I was seriously gonna fetch deh cops on deh idiot.

JAMIE: Don't you fuckin' be at d'at, missus. (*Beat.*) He was pro'lly just drunk.

BEV: Dare say.

JAMIE: All d'at suspense…

BEV: Don't know how he got deh number, mind yuh.

JAMIE: Yuh builds it up and builds it up—

BEV: Sorry b'y.

JAMIE: And it's ol' Art'ur Pretty

BEV: Can't control who calls yuh, b'y.

JAMIE: Well, I'll tell yuh right now—if it wus up tuh me, d'is little piece uh gear right here might be givin' me uh ring.

He points to a girlie poster attached to the bar.

BEV: Go blow yerself.

JAMIE: Won't do no such t'ing. And mind yer mout', girl. You been watchin' too much uh Dad's satellite dish.

BEV: Well, if it wadn't fur yer mudder's salt pork and moose steaks every bejesus time I comes 'ere, I might have d'at girl's abs.

JAMIE: Might take uh few 'ail Marys too, I t'inks.

BEV: Bring me mah drink, yuh shithead.

JAMIE: Plus she's all dark and Italian or whatever.

BEV: She's uh Paki.

JAMIE: *(Double beat.)* Oh. (*Beat.*) Ei'der way.

BEV: Me drink!

JAMIE: Yuh, yuh. Ready to go, yuh townie sourpuss.

BEV: Time don't do nothin' for d'at fishy smell yuh got, b'y.

JAMIE returns to the bar and retrieves a spray can of cologne.

JAMIE: Loud and clear, me dear.

He sprays himself to a ludicrous degree with cologne.

BEV: Don't, b'y! Stop! God, man, yer gonna make deh place smell like fuckin' At'lete's World.

JAMIE: Whiff of uh sportsman, me lovely.

He sprays his bag just as excessively.

BEV: Oh me sweet Jesus. Knows I idn't rotted—

JAMIE throws the can in a wastebasket. Used. It. All. They sit together again.

JAMIE: *(Lighting another cigarette.)* How's deh Black 'Orse?

BEV: Right bad, Jamie. I can't drink d'is piss tuh save me life.

JAMIE: Well, d'ey don't make it in pineapple er pomegranate, hey b'y.

BEV: I needs a Pepsi…

JAMIE: Bev. *No.*

BEV moves to the bar to fetch a Pepsi. She finds a can and sacrilegiously mixes it and some of her beer in a tall glass.

JAMIE: Where deh hell did d'at come from?

BEV: I keeps a stash here 'cause Coke tastes like *oldness.*

JAMIE: Yuh knows I 'ates it when yuh fucks wit' me beer.

BEV: I loves it.

JAMIE: It's like puttin' ketchup on uh good roast.

BEV: I does d'at too.

JAMIE: D'at's me point.

BEV: Peeeerfect.

JAMIE: How deh hell did ol' Art call me anyways? Art don't got no phone. Don't have no house for Chrissake. (*Beat.*) Probably wanted to go fishin' tamarrow.

BEV: It was weird, d'ough.

JAMIE: Wha'?

BEV: He kept askin' about—

A knock at the door.

JAMIE: By deh geeeeeezzzzus.

BEV: It's past twelve-t'irty, Jamie! Yuh knows yuh can't have nobody over d'is late.

JAMIE: Only one stunned arse in town drunk and 'omeless enough tuh be 'ere now.

BEV: You t'inks it's Art?

More knocking.

JAMIE: What wus he wantin'?

BEV: He was slurrin', b'y. Askin' somet'ing about he's niece.

JAMIE: Wha'?

BEV: Ol' Chisel Lips—

More knocking.

JAMIE: Yuh sure?

BEV: I dunno, b'y. Couldn't follow 'em a'tall.

More knocking.

JAMIE: D'is'll be good.

BEV: Oh mah god, Jamie. It's too late—

JAMIE: Look, I'm 'iding deh booze. He'll be best kind.

BEV: But really now—

JAMIE: He's uh hurtin' old drunk, missus.

JAMIE is back at the bar, hiding bottles. He chugs his drink.

I'll let 'em have he's word.

BEV: Fishin' buddies code or somet'in'.

JAMIE: Somet'in', yuh.

JAMIE walks towards the door. There's still light knocking.

BEV: See wha's on deh go but don't be invitin'em in. Freaks me right out he do.

JAMIE: Well, I ain't askin' deh feller in for no Ouija board sleepover or nudding.

BEV: Drunk arsehole t'inks we're open late like uh goddamn Wendy's.

JAMIE: Shoosh. I hears yuh.

JAMIE swings the door open.

Listen, b'y!

JAMIE's tongue is tranquilized as soon as the door opens.

BEV: *(Knitting.)* Just gonna stand d'ere wit' deh door open—? Yer lettin' out deh heat, fishy. (*Beat.*) JAMIE! HEAT!—LOSING IT! CLOSE DEH DOOR!

JAMIE allows the person in. She walks forward and JAMIE shuts the door. The new girl seems unsurprised by JAMIE's quiet show of surprise, and soon looks to BEV, who has been facing the other way, knitting.

DOREEN: Bev?

BEV: *(Turning around.)* Art'ur?

DOREEN: No—

BEV: You ain't Art—

DOREEN: He's a little wider than me, if I recall.

BEV: DODI! Oh mah holy— DODI PRETTY!

DOREEN: How are you, Bev?

BEV: (*Getting up to hug DOREEN.*) I'm—I'm right surprised, like.

DOREEN: Very nice to see you again.

BEV: I dare say! Lard almighty, I 'asn't seen you in ages, sure!

DOREEN: I know. I overdid my hiatus a bit.

BEV: Yer wha'? (*Beat.*) Geez b'y, we wus jus' talkin' 'bout'cha.

DOREEN: Really?

BEV: Yeees, somebody brought yuh up earlier on today, and now here yuh is, hey b'y.

DOREEN: There's a lot of chance in the world, isn't there?

BEV: Jamie! It's Dodi, sure! Dodi Pretty!

DOREEN: No one's called me that in years.

BEV: Yuh don't say! Mainlanders don't get nudding, mah girl.

DOREEN: (*Laughing.*) I've been living no-frills for a while. Doreen everywhere but here.

BEV: Don't suit yuh, sure. Y'er a Dodi if I ever seen one.

DOREEN: I don't think there's a surplus—

BEV: Jamie! Say hello tuh Dodi!

JAMIE: (*Reluctantly.*) Hey Dodi.

DOREEN: How've you been, Jamie?

JAMIE: Right on.

BEV: "Hey Dodi." "Right on." Some manners on yuh, Jamie! I'll get rid uh d'is knittin' stuff and yuh can 'ave a seat, Dodi—

DOREEN: Oh, you don't have to.

BEV: Nah stayin'?

DOREEN: Well—

BEV: Yes, yes. Stay for some tea, girl. I t'inks we still got some Carnation Milk left in deh cupboard.

DOREEN: Oh, no thanks.

BEV: Oh yuh. Gettin' right late for tea. Make'er up uh

Black 'Orse and Pepsi d'en, Jamie. Sit down, would yuh.

DOREEN: I don't really drink.

BEV: Don't drink she says! Well Lard Christ—d'at's 'ow y'er so skinny.

DOREEN: (*Laughing*.) Thank you.

BEV: Yuh looks wicked.

DOREEN: That's sweet of you. You're fabulous yourself.

BEV: Oh, I looks like shit. Jamie tells me all deh time.

JAMIE: No I never.

BEV: Yuh must look at deh back uh every grocery box and eat just deh right servin'. Don't she look good, Jamie? (*Beat*.) Yuh dumb or wha', b'y? Get deh woman a regular ol' Pepsi d'en. She don't drink liquor.

DOREEN: I'm fine, really—

BEV: Scrawny arse don't want regular. Get 'er one uh yer mudder's Diet Cokes from upstairs d'en—

DOREEN: Actually, I—

BEV: OK, OK. No drink. What's on deh go?

DOREEN: On the go. I almost forgot that you guys say that.

BEV: Whattaya at back here on deh Rock fur?

JAMIE: Bev—

BEV: Oh, uh course. I'm some sorry. Yer mudder.

DOREEN: Yes.

BEV: Terrible way tuh go.

DOREEN: Yes it is.

BEV: *Tit cancer*. Fuck, it's gonna get us all.

JAMIE: It's breast cancer, Bev, yuh brute.

BEV: Yuh yuh—she knows what I means.

DOREEN: Of course. No, it's—it's OK.

JAMIE: Does Art'ur know yer home?

DOREEN: Not yet. I tried calling the house to let him know, but the number was unavailable. He must have changed it at some point.

JAMIE: I don't t'ink so.

DOREEN: Pardon?

JAMIE: He didn't switch no numbers.

DOREEN: I called 592-

JAMIE: 2515. (*Beat.*) Yuh.

DOREEN: You remember.

JAMIE: I remembers.

BEV: D'at's crazy. Yer usually crap wit' numbers, Jamie.

DOREEN: I ended up resorting to surface mail.

JAMIE: You haven't been in yer house yet?

DOREEN: No. I rented a car in St. John's and was just driving in— I don't know. I saw your basement light on. I didn't think you'd be here—figured it was your little sister or something—but I wanted to try. I mean, I'm sorry. You were probably getting to bed.

BEV: Jamie just got off work, act'chully.

DOREEN: This late?

BEV: Yes, girl. Dick pickin' hours is deh shits—

JAMIE: Hush up, Bev.

DOREEN: *What* picking?

JAMIE: Bake apples.

BEV: *Dicks*. Sortin' t'rough capelin cocks. Fish plant work, m'dear.

DOREEN: Oh.

BEV: Jamie took it up nah long ago. He wus partners wit' he's dad in deh water sprinkler business before, but he give it up.

JAMIE: Bev, go to bed.

BEV: No way. Not wit' Dodi here fur the first time since grade— what was it, twelve?

DOREEN: Ten.

BEV: All deh more reason to stay and gab a bit. Whattaya been doin' wit' yerself?

DOREEN: I'm in law school, actually.

BEV: Really! What a brain on yuh.

DOREEN: Waited a while. Worked. Traveled.

JAMIE: (*Critically*.) Traveled?

DOREEN: Not a lot.

BEV: Where'd yuh go to?

DOREEN: Well, I was a waitress in Amsterdam just after high school. And I lived in Iceland for a few months more recently…teaching. But yeah, there are some other thirty-ish people in the law program. It makes it a little less alienating.

BEV: Whoa, man—and using deh proper English, too. *Alienationing*, Jamie. Hear d'at?

JAMIE: Bev, go to bed. I got somet'in' tuh tell Dodi.

BEV: Like wha'?

JAMIE: I got somet'ing tuh tell 'er 'bout deh house.

DOREEN: Oh. I heard the news soon after Mom passed.

JAMIE: Yuh did?

BEV: Yer kiddin'.

DOREEN: Well...I inherited the house. (*Beat.*) Right? (*Beat.*)

BEV: Yuh, my bedtime is long past. I gotta drive out town bright and early.

DOREEN: Sorry I kept you up.

BEV: No big deal, girl. Hey, I works at a beauty parlor, Dodi. If yer ever in town and yuh wants yer toes or hair done, or yuh needs uh wax...

JAMIE: Bev. Bed.

BEV hugs DOREEN again.

BEV: Some good seein' yuh. See yuh soon, I'm sure. (*Whispering a bit.*) An' really—if yuh ever needs a Brazilian or anyt'ing— I won't tell no one.

JAMIE: BEV!

BEV: G'night, girl. See yuh in a few minutes, Jamie?

JAMIE: Yuh.

BEV grabs her drink and leaves for the bedroom.

DOREEN: What's going on, Jamie?

JAMIE: Well—

DOREEN: Did something happen? Is Uncle Art OK?

JAMIE: Yuh, Art'ur's fine. I guess.

DOREEN: What do you mean? How did he take the news?

JAMIE: I don't say he took it too good.

DOREEN: Has he been—?

JAMIE: Oh yuh. Plastered on amber rum ever since.

DOREEN: God.

JAMIE: Look, Dodi—

DOREEN: I'm sorry I came. I didn't know Bev would— I didn't know.

JAMIE: Not now, luh.

DOREEN: I'm sorry that I'm twelve years late. I know that's very late.

JAMIE: Dudn't matter—

DOREEN: Aren't you anything more than surprised to see me?

JAMIE: No. I'm jus' surprised. Now please shut up and let me—

DOREEN: Do you hate me?

JAMIE: (*Silent, then throwing up the words.*) Dodi, yer uncle burnt down yer house.

DOREEN: What—?

JAMIE: Yer 'ouse. Yer Chapel 'ouse. It's gone. I know d'at's a lot. Yer mom gone and now d'is. But he did it. He burnt it down. And he wadn't slick about it like he wus when he burnt he's own place. No grease fire d'is time. Deh fuckin' idiot drowned deh place in gasuhline. Bunch uh Williamses up deh road even saw deh dumb arse up on he's roof, crying he's face off and emptying out a gas can. (*Beat.*) I know d'at's a lot.

Scene 2

Wednesday at 1:45am. Chapel Arm, Newfoundland. A small clearing in the woods far behind the black ruins of DOREEN's childhood home. DOREEN and JAMIE stop at a large tent. JAMIE's drinking a beer.

JAMIE: D'ere. D'at's it.

JAMIE lights a cigarette.

DOREEN: Thanks.

JAMIE moves to leave.

"Dat's it," and you leave?

JAMIE: 'Ere. (*Hands her his flashlight.*) I knows me way back—

DOREEN: Jamie.

JAMIE: Dodi, it's two in deh mornin'. Yuh can keep deh light. Best I can do fur yuh.

DOREEN: I guess you gotta get your sleep.

JAMIE: G'night.

DOREEN: You know, rest up so you can get back to pickin'—

JAMIE: I swear tuh God, if I 'ears d'at one more time—

DOREEN: It'll be hard to avoid if you're doing it forty hours a week.

JAMIE: Best uh luck in law school, me ducky.

DOREEN: (*Softly.*) I don't care where you work.

JAMIE: N'eider do I.

DOREEN: Jamie, what if he's not in there?

JAMIE: He don't go nowhere else.

DOREEN: Are you sure?

JAMIE: He don't go nowhere else I says.

DOREEN: Tomorrow. Can we—

JAMIE: Sorry 'bout yer mudder.

DOREEN: Can we?

JAMIE: Dodi…deh answer's no.

DOREEN: Why did I even come here then?

JAMIE: You tell me.

DOREEN: You don't care that somebody *killed* my house.

JAMIE: He made a mistake.

DOREEN: So did I! I sold Mom's house in Toronto. I moved out of my apartment. Out of my plush, almost affordable downtown apartment.

JAMIE: What'd yuh do d'at fur?

DOREEN: To come back here.

JAMIE: Wha'?

DOREEN: (*Chagrined.*) To live.

JAMIE: You wus gonna live in Chapel?

DOREEN: Yes. For awhile at least.

JAMIE: I t'ought you wus gonna be a lawyer.

DOREEN: I don't know.

JAMIE: Well, yuh can't really live 'ere. Jesus Christ.

DOREEN: I couldn't settle on anything else to do.

JAMIE: So now d'at yer bored, yuh t'ought yuh'd just kick Art'ur outta he's 'ouse.

DOREEN: No.

JAMIE: Yer mudder left him 'ere tuh rot, and now—

DOREEN: Don't talk about my mom.

JAMIE: Fine. (*Beat.*) *You* left him 'ere.

DOREEN: We left him *with a house*, Jamie. We gave him our home as a *gift* to replace his own. You know, the *first* one that he *burnt*.

JAMIE: Dodi, he's wife killed 'erself. Maybe scorchin' he's 'ouse wadn't deh proper response, but deh man didn't know what tuh do wit he's self.

DOREEN: It was his fault.

JAMIE: You're outta of line, girl.

DOREEN: I get victimized by a drunken arsonist, and I'm out of line?

JAMIE: STOP ACTIN' LIKE YOU LOST MORE D'AN YER MUDDER.

DOREEN: What?

JAMIE: You lost yer mudder. Dat's tragic. Dat's—my sympat'ies fur it. But Dodi, deh house d'at burnt down wadn't yers.

DOREEN: I meant to come back, you know.

JAMIE: But it was one uh d'ose t'ings yuh never gets around to, right?

DOREEN: It's not that easy to make time.

JAMIE: (*Galled.*) Yuh has time for deh Main*land* and Hol*land* and even fuckin' Ice*land*. But dudn't even pass t'rough Newfound*land*.

DOREEN: I wanted to.

JAMIE: But yuh had tuh wait till now? (*Beat.*) 'Til right now.

DOREEN: What do you mean?

JAMIE: (*Fetching his car keys.*) Never mind. (*Taking a swig of beer.*) Bye Dodi.

DOREEN: Jamie. You've been—

JAMIE: (*Jingling his keys.*) Welcome back to deh Rock, me girl.

JAMIE polishes off his beer while exiting.

DOREEN: I can get your light back to you tomorr—

JAMIE's out. DOREEN makes her way over to the tent and eventually taps her knuckle against it.

What am I doing here? (*Beat.*) You can't knock on a tent.

She kneels beside the tent, listening. She reaches into her coat pocket and throws down some keys, a stick of deodorant, and a cell phone. She finds a pink lighter, clicks a flame into existence, and holds it up teasingly near the tent. ART, 66, steps out from shadowy evergreens.

ART: Dodi.

DOREEN: (*Lowering the lighter.*) Hi. (*Beat.*) Were you here the whole time?

ART: I got yer letter, Dodi. Got it uh couple days ago. Look, I wanted tuh let yuh know 'bout what 'appened—what I let 'appen. It's just d'at I don't get 'round tuh too much, really. Not d'ese days. I should'a done somet'ing. Let yuh know. D'is idn't fair to yuh. I wanted tuh at least get yuh a lift from deh airport. Me car's been dead for eight mont's now. I wadn't ever insured tuh drive it in deh first place, mind yuh, but…anyways. Yesterday I left deh tent fur deh first time in a good long time, hey b'y. Headed over to me buddy Neddy's. He's deh same brud d'at got me yer letter from deh post office. You remembers Neddy Warren, dudn't yuh?

DOREEN: His wife had a poodle.

ART: Ex-wife. And deh poodle's dead now—t'ank God. I went over tuh Neddy's tuh use he's telephone. Wanted d'at Jamie Jr. on deh line, see if he'd pick yuh up at deh airport. Neddy had a sixty-sixer uh Lambs on he's kitchen table, d'ough, so I didn't make out too good.

DOREEN: Thanks.

ART: Sad trut' is d'at I just woke up 'bout 'alf an hour ago. I'm some worthless tuh do d'at to yer family 'ome, and d'en tuh just pass out. I loves yer mudder. Wit'out her…I'd uh been dead years ago. And now—now she's gone. I wanted 'er tuh come visit me some bad. I wanted to see 'er—and you. By deh Jesus, I wanted yuh tuh come 'ome out've it. So I could t'ank you fur lettin' me live 'ere. Givin' me uh 'ome. Givin' me *yer* 'ome. Yuh's left me uh wonderful t'ing… an' it's gone 'cause uh me. Go ahead. Burn me tent. I owes yuh d'at and more.

DOREEN: Jamie told me you never left it.

ART: Well, I 'asn't been, but like I say—'old on! Lard fuckin' Jesus! You t'ought you wus burnin' me! I needs uh cigarette—! Fuckin' crazy arse over 'ere!

DOREEN: Well.

ART: (*Lighting a cigarette.*) Yuh crazy arse—! I burnt uh 'ouse yuh hadn't used in ten years! Not *you*.

DOREEN: I wasn't going to burn your tent for godssake. It was just sort of compelling to hold up the lighter and think.

ART: T'ink wha'?

DOREEN: About where you might be hiding.

ART: Wha'?

DOREEN: You were watching.

ART: Go on, b'y.

DOREEN: You could never lie when you were hung-over.

ART: I wus just waitin' fur a good time tuh talk to yuh.

DOREEN: You came out because you thought I might burn your tent.

ART: I came out tuh talk to yuh. I means it.

DOREEN: I don't trust you.

ART: I don't blame yuh, missus. I'm sorry fur makin' yuh feel d'at way. I'll make it up to yuh, I promise yuh d'at. (*Beat.*) Just as well yuh didn't burn me tent, d'ough. Yuh needs a place to sleep, don't yuh?

DOREEN: No.

ART: Please, Dodi. It's deh least I can do. We'll get

ourselves uh fire goin' if yuh wants. Warm up and trade us some stories. 'Member 'ow I used tuh tell ye's 'bout—

DOREEN: (*Pretty much panicked.*) Guy Fawkes. Yes. Look, I'll just drive back to town. I don't feel good about any of this. I was going to stay, but—

ART: It's late, Dodi.

DOREEN: I'm fine.

DOREEN goes to leave.

ART: I miss 'er too, Dodi. I loved 'er. She treated me like 'er kid and I wadn't—I wus 'er big brudder. (*Beat.*) D'ere's a sleepin' bag in d'ere for yuh.

DOREEN: I can't.

ART: Now what would uh happened tuh Guy Fawkes if he jus' said, "I can't"?

DOREEN: Well… he probably wouldn't have been executed.

ART: And he would uh never got into no 'istory books.

DOREEN: I don't know why I came.

ART: Welcome 'ome, me dear. We Newfies always comes 'ome. I loves yuh. You knows d'at, right?

DOREEN: I know, Uncle Art.

ART: Yuh've always known d'at, right?

DOREEN: I have.

ART: Luh—if yuh stays, we'll get up first t'ing tamarrow and get us uh breakfast feed. I don't got much supplies here—I s'ppose we'll have tuh go tuh Charlotte's. Jus' like old times, hey girl.

DOREEN: I don't think you should be making public appearances.

ART: No one at deh coffee shop's gonna rat on me, b'y.

DOREEN: You don't know that.

ART: I don't see wha' anybody would want wit' me. I was livin' in deh 'ouse. Not like I wus tryin' to kill no one.

DOREEN: Most of the town probably thinks you're dangerous.

ART: Ain't no one pressing charges 'gainst me, is d'ur?

DOREEN: No one needs to press charges. (*Speedily: businesslike at first, and then emotionally overcome.*) Even if you owned the property—and you technically didn't—you could still be looking at up to fourteen years imprisonment for endangering the safety and property of your neighbors. Not to mention the boundless supply of trees that faced each side of the house. (*Almost breathlessly.*) What were you thinking?

ART: (*Bemused.*) Wadn't no one livin' in deh trees.

DOREEN: Wildlife, Uncle Art.

ART: What odds. Sure ev'ryone 'round 'ere be's shootin' deh fucking squirrels anyways.

DOREEN: Fourteen years, Uncle Art.

ART: Faurteen years. Lard dyin'.

DOREEN: You're lucky.

ART: I wouldn't say d'at. All I been eatin' is berries. D'ey goes right t'rough me, hey b'y.

DOREEN: Great.

ART: I is what I is.

DOREEN: You are what you are.

ART: Hey b'y.

ART pulls out his cigarettes. He secures one for himself, and then gestures to DOREEN with the pack.

DOREEN: No thanks.

ART: Good girl. Yuh passed deh test.

DOREEN: In that case, I will take one.

ART: Don't be at d'is nonsense, Dodi.

DOREEN: Well, I wouldn't usually. You owe me and I'm pretty at peace with the idea of killing myself to spite you.

ART: 'Ere yuh go d'en.

He hands her a cigarette. It goes in her mouth, Art lights it for her, and she puffs like a rookie.

No wonder it burnt down, y'know, wit' deh volunteer firefighters we got. Bunch uh fuckin' pogey collectin' fishermen drunk an' stoned goin' mad wit' hoses.

DOREEN: Yeah. (*Beat.*) You and Jamie. Do you still hang out?

ART: I likes tuh see deh guy when I can. Er, well, when he can, I guess.

DOREEN: Here?

ART: Yeah… and we goes on troutin' trips every now an' d'en. Jamie Jr.'s pretty much deh only buddy I be's happy to see nowadays. Ever since Neddy got remarried to d'at Protestant slut.

DOREEN: Remember when you'd pick us up from school?

ART: Ev'ry Wednesday at noon, me dear. Ye's loved yer Charlotte's takeout.

DOREEN: We were always late getting back. Mom got so cross with you for that.

ART: She was deh funniest angry person. She'd squint right hard atcha like yuh was ten centimeters big. Deh "T'ree Blind Mice" she called us.

DOREEN: You're still his friend. I can't believe it. Maybe because I don't think I am.

ART: Go on wit'cha. Young Bev pro'lly had 'em drove nuts by deh time yuh seen 'em. Dat Bev's uh hard ticket d'at is.

DOREEN: How so?

ART: Well, I don't wanna get too into it— (*Beat.*) She makes 'em have t'reesomes.

DOREEN: What?

ART: T'reesomes.

DOREEN: You're kidding.

ART: No. She's uh quare bitch.

DOREEN: He doesn't like it?

ART: I don't know. Dudn't seem to. Not no more anyways.

DOREEN: Wow. I thought that used to be a male fantasy or something.

ART: Oh, still is. Still is fur most uh us.

DOREEN: Well, even Bev was more responsive to me tonight. And she loathed me when I lived here. She used to call me Chisel Lips. She equated these (*Indicating her lips.*) with a steel wedge-like tool that I pulled out of Jamie's garage as a kid so I could compare it with my mouth—

ART: D'at bucktoot' pregnant raptor. Never seen deh likes of 'er.

DOREEN: *Pregnant*...raptor?

ART: She got eyes like uh fuckin' raptor, Dodi. Don't even say she don't.

DOREEN: OK. But—?

ART: Oh. Jamie never said nudding?

DOREEN: She's *pregnant*?

ART: Yuh. Jus' found out a few weeks ago, I t'inks.

DOREEN: She likes *girls*. And she's carrying *his* baby.

ART: Ain't fit, wha'?

DOREEN: Did he hate me right away? That first year?

ART: Don't make no diff'rence now.

DOREEN: Has he hated me for twelve years? Is that what I'm dealing with?

ART: He got real excited deh first t'ree or faur. D'en he jus'—

DOREEN: I miss him. I miss how he was.

ART: And how you wus?

DOREEN: I wanted to come back and see him. See you. See Chapel. Every year. You have to know that was the plan.

ART: Don't need tuh esplain yerself tuh me, girl.

DOREEN: But I was scared of coming here.

ART: I knows.

DOREEN: Mom told me I wasn't allowed. That sounds weak, but she made the place seem Third World.

ART: I'm sorry tuh hear d'at.

DOREEN: I literally couldn't make it here.

ART: I believes yuh.

DOREEN: It was because of you.

ART: I knows I was uh terrible embarrassment to 'er—

DOREEN: Don't.

ART: Wha'?

DOREEN: You know what.

ART: No b'y—

DOREEN: I remember, OK.

ART: I t'inks it's time yuh got some rest, girl—

DOREEN: No.

ART: Yes, Dodi, before d'is gets out uh hand—

DOREEN: I remember why Aunt Loretta killed herself.

ART: Don't be talkin' about me wife. Please Dodi.

DOREEN: Fine.

DOREEN stares daringly at her uncle, giving him a moment to think, "She wouldn't," but then she does, grabbing the back of his head and pulling him into an ill-tempered kiss of biting and bliss and storied taboo. ART initially resists out of guilt, but then he squeezes his niece's leg and loses some fingers in her hair.

I think I missed you.

ART: I loves you. I still loves you.

They walk calmly into the tent, saying nothing. Once inside, ART turns on a large flashlight that illuminates the tent, silhouetting ART and DOREEN.

Scene 3

Thursday at 7:45 PM, the following week. Chapel Arm. A swim-worthy pool on the north end of a small river. JAMIE is wearing old rubber boots and standing about calf high in the shallow end of the pool. He holds a long and conspicuously sophisticated spinning rod. He casts it out, waits a tick, reels slightly, and then jerks the rod.

JAMIE: Gimme uh nibble now, b'ys.

Reel, reel, jerk.

C'mon and give us uh bite, yuh l'il pink-bellied, pan-fry fuckers.

He reels and notices a tug. He jerks. Bingo. He reels just a little too eagerly and—bad bingo.

Yuh dirty cunt!

As he reels the line in for another cast, DOREEN appears above JAMIE on a rickety wooden lookout at the end of a boggy walking trail. She partially hears the end of JAMIE's mumblings, which prompts her to look down at the water.

DOREEN: What are you saying down there?

JAMIE isn't expecting a visitor—let alone one with DOREEN's voice—so the surprise sabotages his next cast of line. The line whips to the water immediately in front of his feet, giving JAMIE the appearance of a small boy on his first fishing excursion.

JAMIE: Shit!

DOREEN: Sorry.

JAMIE: Yuh.

JAMIE takes several watery steps away from DOREEN's platform.

DOREEN: Look. About Uncle Art—

JAMIE: Don't bodder, Dodi.

DOREEN: I know it's bad.

JAMIE: What odds.

DOREEN: I've spent most of my recent time synthesizing really poignant things to say to you.

JAMIE: Right on.

DOREEN: The rest of the time I just spent thinking you wouldn't want to listen anyway.

JAMIE: Oh yuh.

DOREEN: Will you?

JAMIE: Yuh should uh never took 'em d'ere.

DOREEN: I didn't want to. He—

JAMIE: Ye's should'a never been d'ere. Yuh knows damn well yuh shouldn'tuh been.

DOREEN: I know. I told him that it [was a bad idea]—

JAMIE: I t'ought you wus some kind uh lawyer.

DODI: (*Quietly.*) Yes.

JAMIE: Remin' me not tuh ask yuh for no legal advice.

DOREEN: He wanted to go. He decided to go. You know how much sense that man makes.

JAMIE: Funny. He's deh one d'at don't make sense, but yer deh one I dudn't understand.

DOREEN: I'm sorry I didn't try harder to stop him. I did try, but—

JAMIE: No yuh never. Or else he wudn't be locked up right now, scared tuh deat'.

DOREEN: You're right.

JAMIE: Fulish prick tried tuh get me tuh Charlotte's half uh dozen times, but we never went d'ere. Don't need no diplomas tuh figure out d'at idn't gonna work.

DOREEN: You're right. (*Beat.*) Is the water still good?

JAMIE: Wha'?

DOREEN: Is it deep? Still good for swimming?

JAMIE: (*Distantly.*) 'Bout twelve feet in deh center.

DOREEN: Things have grown in, but nicely.

JAMIE: Nudding bitin' here.

JAMIE starts a slow walk on slippery rocks around the edge of the water body. His line remains a few feet from him; he pulls it gently behind him.

DOREEN: (*Shouting like it's the last time she'll see him.*) Don't you want to know what I'm doing, Jamie? Where I've been living for the last week? What I'm eating? *If* I'm eating!

JAMIE: Yuh looks decent enough.

DOREEN: Don't you want to know what I did for the last TWELVE YEARS?

JAMIE: Not if yer gonna scare all deh fish off, b'y.

DOREEN: I just mean…

DOREEN uses her next bulk of lines to walk down a shoddy collection of steps. She settles on the last step.

Can't we talk? Can't we have a *conservation*?

JAMIE won't let himself smile, but he does shake his head about as playfully as his pride will allow, recognizing her allusion. He may walk closer to DOREEN in the next few minutes.

Remember how you used to say that when we were little? Whenever you thought it was time to put the plastic kitchen appliances away, you'd sit down somewhere, pat the spot beside you and say, "Dooooodiii… come 'ere, we has uh *conservation*."

JAMIE: I knows I wadn't deh smartest brat out d'ere. Still idn't, tuh tell yuh deh trut'.

DOREEN: I didn't have the heart to correct you.

JAMIE: I ended up gettin' told so many times in elem'try school I just gave up tryin' to say boat words.

DOREEN: I noticed. (*Beat.*) So?

JAMIE: I dunno.

DOREEN: Come on. Talk to me.

JAMIE nods his head.

Good.

DOREEN's waiting for JAMIE to go first. JAMIE does not want to go first.

JAMIE: Yeeeees b'y.

DOREEN: You can't think of anything to say to me?

JAMIE: Whattaya want?

DOREEN: For you to say one scrap of a thing that isn't crabby conversational fodder.

JAMIE: I didn't say nudding 'bout yer fodder.

DOREEN: Look at where we are, Jamie. Big Tunnel.

JAMIE: So wha'?

DOREEN: We must have gone swimming here five hundred times.

JAMIE: And prob'ly five t'ounsand times since yuh left. D'at's deh t'ing, Dodi. Yes, we wus good buddies and we had some deadly times…but you chose tuh give it up.

DOREEN: Remember that big misfire we had jumping off the rocks the first summer we came here? (*Pointing.*) You were on the highest (*She indicates the platform above.*) and I was on the second highest (*The other side of the stage.*) …and you hadn't seen me leap from the rock…

JAMIE: No, girl. It was deh second summer we come here. Deh first summer you wus too scared tuh jump off anyt'ing.

DOREEN: Really?

JAMIE: Yes, you said yer mudder wadn't fussy 'bout you jumpin' off deh big 'eights. 'Fraid yuh'd get yer brains damaged er somet'in. Prob'ly true, but yuh knows yuh would uh jumped anyway if yuh'd wanted to.

DOREEN: Probably.

JAMIE: And it wudn't d'at I didn't see you goin'. I called it—I said, "I'm jumpin', Dodi—'old up!" But you wus freakin' out 'bout Uncle Art bein' unnwadder. Here he wus lookin' fur fish with he's scuba goggles on, and you t'ought he was drowned er somet'ing.

DOREEN: Oh yeah.

JAMIE: 'Ad tuh jump off and save 'em. Nearly killed all t'ree of us.

DOREEN: You didn't land on us though.

JAMIE: Swerved over to deh side as much as I could. Landed wit' a big ol' Johnny Ass Cracker in deh shallow end—

DOREEN: I hated those.

JAMIE: Wadn't too pleasant, girl. And as much as it cracked yer arse, it wadn't kind on its two neighbours neid'er, hey b'y.

DOREEN: (*Laughing.*) I'm sorry.

JAMIE: Anyway. Best be goin', Dodi.

DOREEN: Why?

JAMIE: I can't treat yuh deh same as I did.

DOREEN: Not the same, then—just familiar.

JAMIE: Yuh ain't familiar tuh me no more.

DOREEN: Jamie, we're here.

JAMIE: Yer way too late, Dodi.

DOREEN: You were always late. You'd say you were coming over for supper at 5:00 and show up at 8:30, wondering if you were allowed the leftovers. I always waited. You were just getting in the shower when I'd show up at your house ready to go to school. I'd run to the bus shelter and hold up the driver.

JAMIE: I t'inks if I had been t'irteen years late fur school, d'ey would'a booted me out, hey.

DOREEN: That's only one way of looking at this.

JAMIE: And what's deh udder one?

DOREEN: I let you down. I really let you down. But by being away, I may have spared us some juvenile misfortunes. What if we got further along in high school and had a falling out or found our way into separate cliques? What if we fell for other people?

JAMIE: It's not like we wus going out or nudding anyways—

DOREEN: You wouldn't have cared if I had lived here and been with someone else?

JAMIE: Yuh knows I would'a gone right savage on deh fucker.

DOREEN: Maybe we would have stopped talking and steered ourselves away from ever being here again.

JAMIE: So I should be grateful d'at you broke yer promise? Yuh—t'anks, Dodi, fur being a liar.

DOREEN: No. But maybe my mistake has some perks. And maybe it's anomalous that we've made it here.

JAMIE: (*Lost.*) OK, if we're gonna talk—

DOREEN: Did I say anomalous? I meant…I meant CRAZY! Yeah, I mean it's…it's CRAZY that we're here talking at length as we are. Acknowledging what we were and how we still think about it. Most people, most childhood friends…don't get this. If they don't talk for years, then they never do. Or if they do, it's peripheral—uh, which means on the side, and not very good—

JAMIE: I knows what it means.

DOREEN: Right! And so—sure, such reunions are always courteous, but they almost never allow people to recapture what made them feel notable together in the first place.

JAMIE: But listen to yuh—yer not deh same. Yer Doreen. Not Dodi. Not no more.

DOREEN: Fuck you.

JAMIE: Wha'? (*Beat.*) Did you just swear at me? (*Beat.*) I never 'eard you swear in me life.

DOREEN: Well, there you go. You know something new about me. Something you missed. I do swear sometimes. Not as much as Bev, who sounds like a Trailer Park Boy, but I'll swear when I'm accordingly "rotted" or "poisoned," as it were. Just because there are new things to know about me doesn't mean everything you used to know has been discarded. For instance—what's my favourite food?

JAMIE: Pizza.

DOREEN: YES! Exactly!

JAMIE stares at her, unconvinced.

JAMIE: Deh whole fucking world's favourite food is pizza, Dodi.

DOREEN: The point is…it's consistent. You knew me when my favourite food was pizza. And now here I am, and my favourite food's still pizza. I'm more about spinach and feta now than Uncle Art's infamous chopped hotdog and beer recipe. So my taste has changed, but it's still pretty much the same if you look at the base ingredients. (*Beat.*) Am I Pepsi or Coke?

JAMIE: Coca-Cola, b'y.

DOREEN: Diet nowadays, but yes. And you're a Coke man too.

JAMIE: 'Til deh day I dies.

DOREEN: And what about me and fishing?

JAMIE: Well, you wudn't too hot at it.

DOREEN: And that's still true today. But in addition to sucking at it, I'm now kind of morally opposed to it.

JAMIE: Oh Lard Christ.

DOREEN: It's selfish.

JAMIE: It's fuckin' delicious.

DOREEN: And my favourite number?

JAMIE: T'ree.

DOREEN: Three, actually. (*She smiles, an adorable jerk.*) But as stated, I do like the environment.

JAMIE: Piss off.

DOREEN: And why three?

JAMIE: (*With some hesitation.*) 'Cause uh you, me and Art'ur.

DOREEN: Yes.

JAMIE: Wha's changed 'bout d'at one?

DOREEN: Not much. Nothing, Jamie. Just a cluster of time. (*Beat.*) You know, I never jumped off the highest before I left.

JAMIE: No yuh never.

DOREEN: I've wanted to.

JAMIE: It's kinda like deh second 'ighest, only 'igher.

DOREEN: I want to do it.

JAMIE: Yuh should, b'y.

DOREEN: I want to jump.

JAMIE: Right on.

DOREEN: (*Moving up the steps.*) Off the highest.

JAMIE: I heard yuh, b'y!

DOREEN: I wanna jump *now*!

JAMIE: It's almost October, girl. I don't know 'ow long Lake Ontario er Super'ur er whatever stays fit, but d'is ain't, like, piss warm er nudding.

DOREEN: So what!

JAMIE: So…it's pretty cold.

DOREEN: Can't be that cold.

JAMIE: Well, if deh water idn't freezin' nuff fur yuh, the wind ought'a put deh fear uh Jack Frost up yer arse.

DOREEN: We're just jumping in for a splash.

JAMIE: Oh we is, is we? What are yuh—me mudder?

DOREEN: Yes. Jamie Gerard Griffiths! Get up these stairs and—

DOREEN pulls him up the stairs with one arm. She may start to pull up her shirt with the other, which is eventually cleared with that arm and the other, newly freed arm. After a few pulled steps, JAMIE will hesitantly cooperate and walk upwards unassisted until he realizes DOREEN is topless, left with a bra, and hastily unfastening and pulling down her pants.

JAMIE: You ain't me mudder, b'y.

DOREEN: I didn't bring a bathing suit.

JAMIE: 'Oly Jesus, Dodi!

DOREEN: What?

JAMIE: Why are yuh outta yer clothes, missus?!

DOREEN: As to keep them dry. We're going swimming.

JAMIE: (*Quartered: guilty, worried, awkward and impressed.*) We're goin' SWIMMING—!

DOREEN: At Big Tunnel.

JAMIE: Ah yes—

DOREEN: Jumping off the highest.

JAMIE: Off deh highest, yes b'y—

DOREEN: Right now.

JAMIE: Currently, she says—

DOREEN: Yes.

JAMIE: I would like you—currently—to get less naked. If d'at makes any sense a'tall.

DOREEN: Less naked?

JAMIE: As in put on yer clothes, yuh mainland floozy.

DOREEN: Is this your typical response to women removing their pants?

JAMIE: Dodi, god love yuh, yer an adult, if yer foolish enough tuh wanna go swimmin', yuh can make d'at decision yer big girl self. Enjoy deh 'Ypot'ermia. Go to 'er, buddy. But I gotta go—

DOREEN: Jamie, you're swimming with me.

JAMIE: Can't be at it.

DOREEN: Come on—

JAMIE: No. Seriously—

DOREEN: Just take off your shirt—

JAMIE: I'M 'AVIN' A BABY, DODI—!

JAMIE tosses back DOREEN's snaky arms harder than he wants to, and the force knocks her onto her bottom. She lands with discomfort; maybe she winces.

I'm sorry.

JAMIE, bewildered, offers DOREEN his hand to help her up.

DOREEN: No. (*As he backs off.*) Thank you.

JAMIE: Bev is 'aving a baby.

JAMIE retreats down the steps with his rod and empty trout basket. He works his way through the rocky brook, eventually out of sight.

DOREEN: I'm living here. I threw my name in at the fish plant. Waiting to hear back about it. I'm here, Jamie. In Chapel. My cousin Geraldine is letting me rent her basement from her. She told me that you and some other guys helped her husband build the place. You did a great job on the hardwood floors.

DOREEN turns her back to the ledge, picks up the clothing she previously shed, and makes for the path that brought her here. A spontaneous pivot has her almost jumping into the brook, but she stops herself. She picks up the clothing again, disappointed.

Scene 4

Friday at 4:30 PM, the next day. Just outside Chapel Arm. A set of steps at the entrance of a lakeside cabin. JAMIE sits with a bottle of Black Horse between his knees. BEV enters.

BEV: Come back in, Jamie. It's uh nice birt'day party. D'ur's presents for yuh.

JAMIE: Fodder 'asn't said nudding tuh me.

BEV: And you 'asn't nudding tuh yer fodder.

JAMIE: Funny 'ow d'at works, hey.

BEV: Grow up, luh.

JAMIE: Piss off, luh.

BEV: He jus' wants yuh tuh live out town so deh business can get at customers quicker.

JAMIE: It's not my business, Bev.

BEV: He wants it to be.

JAMIE: I don't care 'bout sprinklers.

BEV: But yuh cares 'bout pickin' t'rough fish cocks wit' bingo ladies?

JAMIE: I loves it.

BEV: No yuh don't.

JAMIE: At least deh fish ain't Fodder's. And at least de're 'ere and not out town.

BEV: Town's just eighty-somet'in clicks away, b'y.

JAMIE: Ain't my place.

BEV: Don't yuh ever wanna move in wit' me? Wit' deh baby?

JAMIE: He's not doing right by me.

BEV: He's only askin' you to leave because—

JAMIE: Nuff said. He's kickin' me out—

BEV: Yuh, and he's right to.

JAMIE: He ain't makin' me do nudding.

BEV: Maybe he ain't…but I am. It's time, man. It's yer twenty-nint' birt'day, y'know. It idn't t'irty. But it's close. You t'ink about d'at.

JAMIE: Yeeees b'y.

BEV: D'ere's more roast if yuh wants it. Yer mudder got deh marble McCain's cake yuh likes wit' deh deadly icin'. She wanted me to say yer fodder got it but she did.

JAMIE: Well, y'knows.

BEV: She said d'at when yer fodder saw us pullin' in deh cabin driveway, he walked by deh mirror on he's bedroom door uh bunch'a times tryin' tuh get he's hair parted right.

JAMIE: He gay or wha'?

BEV: Smarten up. If yer ever gonna be so much better d'an yer makin' yer own fodder out tuh be...you knows what tuh do.

She puts her hands on his shoulders and pulls herself around to kiss him on the cheek. She does.

I loves yuh.

JAMIE: And he do too, right?

BEV: Only if yuh comes back in and eats yer fuckin' McCain's.

JAMIE: I'll be in now deh once.

BEV: Happy birt'day.

BEV returns to the house's interior.

JAMIE sits on the steps.

On the other side of the stage, DOREEN enters the woods where Uncle ART's tent is standing. JAMIE retrieves a squashed paper party hat and puts it on. DOREEN retrieves her uncle's flask and pours the contents onto the ground. JAMIE heads back into the cabin, DOREEN into her tent. A powerful internal light turns the tent into a silhouette box. DOREEN is shown preparing herself and her sleeping bag for an evening under the sky. JAMIE appears in the same woods, barely recognizable in the darkness until he is quite near the tent. He cautiously knocks on the side of the tent. Lights out as DOREEN harshly turns around to recognize the disturbance.

Act II

Scene 1

Friday at 5:32 PM, a pregnancy later. St. John's, Newfoundland. BEV and JAMIE's modest apartment on Water Street. A musing Jamie stands over his son's crib. He's still wearing his blue work coveralls. He leans over the side of the crib, getting a close look at Jamie III.

JAMIE: I dunno what tuh be at, little man. All I ever wanted wus Dodi. Nudding against yer mom—she's a good woman. A real good mudder. She's always decent tuh me. But I wants Dodi. I jus' do. I don't 'ave tuh t'ink about it—it's jus' d'ere. If I 'ad known she wus comin' back, I wouldn't uh done d'is to yer mudder. I wouldn't uh led 'er on, like. But d'en I wouldn't uh 'ad you, right? So I'm standing 'ere now, an'… (*Extending an arm.*) on one side uh me is deh girl who asked me out fur years, deh girl who wanted me more d'en anyone else ever laid eyes on me, deh mudder uh me baby boy. And (*Extending the other.*) on deh udder side is deh girl I wants jus' 'cause I do, just 'cause she's inside uh me. She would uh been deh one memory I'd uh kept if I had to wipe deh works of it. But she came back—she's not just deh girl stuck in me old yearbooks no more. (*Beat.*) D'en d'ere's you…right in deh middle. Wiggling yer little gummy worm fingers. (*Beat.*) Daddy needs a smoke.

JAMIE pulls out a pack and lights the cigarette.

JAMIE: NOT OVER DEH BABY'S CRIB! Jesus, Jamie, yer bad at d'is. Smoke—outside! Smoke—outside! Baby—must—learn—tuh—breed [breathe]! Little Jamie gets cancer at four mont's old and yer gonna look like a fuckin' hard case! Smoke—out—deh—door! Smoke—out—deh—

Just as JAMIE's almost in the clear, BEV arrives home from work and catches him smoking in the house.

BEV: JAMIE!

JAMIE: (*Shuffling outside.*) Hey me darlin'!

They continue hollering at each other with BEV inside, perhaps putting away some things or checking on the baby, and JAMIE just outside the door, smoking.

BEV: What did I say about smokin' in deh house?

JAMIE: I—uh— it ain't permitted—

BEV: And why not?

JAMIE: 'Cause—

BEV: 'Cause it'll kill yer fuckin' only child yuh genius yuh.

JAMIE: Yes, d'at's it. Sorry, me love. (*Beat.*)

BEV: Jamie, whattaya at right now?

JAMIE: Uh…smokin'.

BEV: Why?

JAMIE: 'Cause. I smokes.

BEV: I'm tryin' tuh talk to yuh. Come inside out've it.

JAMIE: But I t'ought I couldn't smoke inside…?

BEV: So put out deh goddamn cig'rette and come 'ere, I talks to yuh.

JAMIE: (*Opening the door, sucking back all he can of the cigarette before discarding it.*) Sounds good, me dear.

BEV has placed her purse and other belongings on the floor. She has her hands on her hips.

JAMIE: Ah Christ, she got 'er 'ands on 'er 'ips.

BEV: Dare say I do.

BEV fetches a pack of gum. She busts out three pieces and sacrifices each one to her mouth, three mice staring down a python's abysmal inner workings.

BEV: Yuh shouldn't be at d'at garbage anyways.

JAMIE: Yes b'y. I should just start chompin' five packs uh gum uh day like you does.

BEV: D'at's better d'an two packs uh what you be's at.

JAMIE: I be's at? You started smokin' when you wus eleven years old fur deh love uh God. You gave me me first cig'rette, sure!

BEV: Don't see me wit' neid'er cig'rette in me mout' now, do yuh?

JAMIE: No—

BEV: And why not?

JAMIE: Because d'en yuh'd be smokin' inside deh 'ouse…an', as we discussed, dat's proh'ited.

BEV: I quit because I had a CHILD.

JAMIE: Yes, I knows—

BEV: And it ain't proper tuh be blowin' nic'uh'tine an' ammonia into deh poor beautiful bugger.

JAMIE: I agrees wit'cha, but—

BEV: D'en give it up. GROW UP. Grow up out've it like I did, mah son, and stop pretendin' d'at smokin' cig'rettes is cool like when yuh 'ung out back uh deh post office in 'igh schoo.

JAMIE: I don't t'ink it's cool.

BEV: D'en find somet'in' else tuh be at.

JAMIE: Like wha'?

BEV: DEH PATCH, fur starters.

JAMIE: I ain't havin' no big ol' bandages on me all deh time.

BEV: Oh, so deh feller who showers twice a week is gettin' vain all of uh sudden.

JAMIE: D'ose patches gives yuh nightmares, Bev. Jase Power told me d'at. He didn't sleep fur t'ree weeks and now he smokes twice as much.

BEV: Mind now.

BEV takes time to uncase and chew another piece of gum.

So wha' movie yuh wanna watch tonight?

JAMIE: Wha'?

BEV: Get deh *Evenin' Telegram* out, we sees what's playin'.

JAMIE: Oh. No, uh—

BEV: Deh paper didn't come again today? D'ose lazy fuckers are gettin' uh piece uh me mind now—

She might make like she's going for a phone. She wouldn't know the number anyway.

JAMIE: No, it come. I gotta go out Chapel fur deh weeken', d'ough.

BEV: Wha'?

JAMIE: Fodder jus' call' me uh few minutes ago. I gotta go 'ave uh look at Matt'ew Jarvis' system in Bellevue.

BEV: Why don't he do it?

JAMIE: He wus goin' to but he and mudder and Nicole went out to deh cabin fur deh weekend an' he forgot he was s'ppose look at it d'is evening. Mudder don't want 'em goin' to Chapel out've it and d'en all deh way back up deh junction. Y'knows, 'cause he's blood pressure.

BEV: Deh junction is uh whole helluva lot closer tuh Chapel d'en we is, hey b'y.

JAMIE: I knows, but he got two or t'ree appointments 'round deh bay early deh tamarrow mornin', too, so he 'llow's I might as well go home an' take care uh it since I ain't got nudding lined up in town fur two-t'ree days.

BEV: D'at sucks, Jamie. It's Friday.

JAMIE: I knows.

BEV: We always sees uh movie on Friday. And Krissy from work wanted tuh come wit' us too.

JAMIE: Yes, I knows, girl.

BEV: Now I'm right disappointed, like. It's me one night tuh 'ave some fun. I be's too tired after me Saturday shift.

JAMIE: Luh—we'll see two movies next Friday d'en.

BEV: Not deh same, mah son.

JAMIE: Best I can do.

BEV: I'm rotted now. Krissy was right excited, like. We 'asn't 'ad her over in a while neider.

JAMIE: Well, what odds about Krissy.

BEV: I t'ought you liked 'anging out wit' 'er.

JAMIE: She's fine, Bev, but I don't wanna be at d'at no more.

BEV: You has fun.

JAMIE: Yer me girlfriend. I shouldn't be messin' round wit' no one but you. Right?

BEV: Don't count as messin' round if I'm d'ere in deh middle uh deh mess.

JAMIE: I guess so.

BEV: Tell yer fodder yuh gotta stay out fur just tonight.

JAMIE: Can't, b'y.

BEV: Jamie, yuh ain't goin' nowhere.

JAMIE: It's jus' business, Bev.

BEV: No way—you wants uh excuse tuh go drinkin' and smokin' all weekend.

JAMIE: No Bev. Jus' business.

BEV: Abandonin' yer wife and child—

JAMIE: Come off it.

BEV: Not even yer wife and child—yer girlfriend and bastard child, 'cause yuh still ain't picked me out uh ring yet eid'er.

JAMIE: Bev.

BEV: Spends eighty bucks uh week on cig'rettes but can't get uh wedding band for he's baby's mudder.

JAMIE: I gotta go. Like I say, it's jus' business.

BEV: Business me arse. We ain't made business in uh good two munt's.

JAMIE: I'll call you when I gets d'ere.

BEV: Oh yuh. I'll be 'ere. Watchin' Sponge Cunt Quare Pants wit' deh youngster.

JAMIE: I'm sorry, Bev.

BEV: Yer comin' back tamarrow d'ough, right?

JAMIE: Act'chully…

BEV: Yer shittin' me.

JAMIE: Sorry.

BEV: Why can't yuh come 'ome out of it tamarrow?

JAMIE: I 'as uh installation in T'ornlee d'at'll take me into deh afternoon. And Edgar Reid needs me tuh take uh look at he's shop around suppertime.

BEV: So yuh can come back tuh town fur deh night.

JAMIE: Well—it's Tommy's birt'day too.

Bev: No it ain't, b'y.

JAMIE: Is, b'y. Landed right on uh Saturday too. Like deh dumb fuck needed uh excuse tuh drink er somet'in.

BEV: Dat's too bad. I would uh liked tuh seen deh brud for he's birt'day. Wus he now? T'irty?

JAMIE: I dunno, Bev. I don't keep track uh d'at racket.

BEV: Maybe I'll give mudder uh call and see if she wouldn't mind me and little Jamie comin' out tamarrow. I ain't been on deh go in deh longest spell.

JAMIE: Yuh…yuh, if yuh wants. Just a few uh deh b'ys going down deh club. Nudding too big. Probably just deh b'ys.

BEV: Yuh don't want me tuh go eid'er, do yuh?

JAMIE: I never said d'at.

BEV: Yes yuh did.

JAMIE: Jus' sayin'—yuh might find it borin', hey b'y.

BEV: I knows what it's like, Jamie. I lived d'ere fur a few years, luh.

JAMIE: Well—it's just gonna be uh bunch uh deh fellers sittin' round drinkin' and shootin' pool. Smokin' cig'rettes between games. You knows.

BEV: Fine d'en.

JAMIE: I'll call yuh later on.

BEV: Do what yuh wants, mah son.

JAMIE reaches into his pants pocket and removes a wad of bills—probably about fifty dollars' worth—which he places in BEV's hand.

JAMIE: Get uh babysitter if yuh still wants tuh go to deh movie. Er rent somet'in if yuh wants.

BEV: Keep it. Don't feel like nudding now.

JAMIE: Please. (*Puts it on a table.*) I feels bad. Do whatever yuh wants. I'm sorry, girl.

BEV: G'night, Jamie.

JAMIE: You too.

JAMIE walks to the door.

BEV: Yuh seen much uh Dodi lately?

JAMIE: Wha'?

BEV: Dodi. Yuh know what she been at?

JAMIE: Got no clue, me love.

BEV: Really?

JAMIE: Ain't seen 'er a'tall.

BEV: I would uh t'ought yuh'd seen 'er when yuh wus out 'round deh bay.

JAMIE: Ain't seen 'er, b'y. Sure she's OK d'ough.

BEV: Well…if yuh sees her, tell 'er I hope she's doin' good.

JAMIE: Fur sure. I mean…if I sees 'er. Fur sure.

BEV: She never come to deh salon.

JAMIE: Wha'?

BEV: I told 'er if she ever needed 'er hair done—

JAMIE: Oh yuh. (*Beat.*) Maybe she's growing it.

BEV: No, she likes hair. Likes lookin' clean. I could tell when I seen 'er last.

JAMIE: Right on. (*Beat.*) Yuh, well see yuh later, all right?

BEV: Watch fur moose.

JAMIE: Uh course. I'll call yuh.

JAMIE grabs a backpack. Then he's gone.

Scene 2

Saturday at 7:13 AM. Chapel Arm. A morning that follows one of JAMIE and DOREEN's numerous evenings spent together. JAMIE and DOREEN manage a dory in the Atlantic, several miles from the nearest Chapel wharf, and a shorter but still significant distance from the shore. Jamie is the oarsman. DOREEN has her hand over the side of the dory, dipping her fingertips in the chilly water. She is fascinated.

DOREEN: Oh! (*Looking down at the water.*) What's that?

JAMIE: Codfish.

DOREEN: Good to know there's still one or two left, huh?

JAMIE: No, he's dead.

DOREEN: Oh.

JAMIE: Yuh worked at deh fish plant all summer and yuh still don't know yer ocean.

DOREEN: Don't need to. It's not like I pick dicks while snorkeling.

JAMIE: Yuh don't have tuh call it d'at. I knows everyone do, but I finds it uh bit shameful.

DOREEN: You don't even pick them anymore, townie.

JAMIE: I means fur you.

DOREEN: Don't get sore. You bailed.

JAMIE: I couldn't very well do d'at fur deh rest uh me life.

DOREEN: Mmhmm. So that meant you had to move an hour away with your wife.

JAMIE: She's not me wife, Dodi. And I kinda had tuh bring 'er wit' me.

DOREEN: Why?

JAMIE: Well, she 'ad me spawn in 'er gut at deh time.

DOREEN: There is that.

JAMIE: (*Putting his ores down.*) D'is looks like a good spot.

DOREEN: How do you know? You got a fish finder over there?

JAMIE: Nah fur fishin'. Crap spot for fishin'. Deadly spot fur drinkin', d'ough.

JAMIE cracks open a Canadian Light and tosses an unopened one to DOREEN.

Real nice spot fur drinkin'. Besides, fishin' is right inhumane, hey b'y.

DOREEN: It is. (*Beat.*) Canadian Light?

JAMIE: I'm nah sayin' it's me favourite. I t'inks Black 'Orse has much more flavor to it. But I can't be on d'at if I'm drinkin' lots. Gets deh big fat gut on me, hey b'y.

DOREEN: You plan on getting drunk with me—out in a boat?

JAMIE: Dodi, I plans on spendin' deh day wit'cha.

DOREEN: What did you tell Bev?

JAMIE: Installations.

DOREEN: You know...she might be into it.

JAMIE: Nah, she hates boats.

DOREEN: Not that.

JAMIE: Whattaya mean d'en?

DOREEN: Why do you always have a case of beer when you're here?

JAMIE: I 'as a case uh beer pretty much wherever I goes.

DOREEN: At work?

JAMIE: I don't install smood'ly until me t'ird bottle's gone.

DOREEN: Dentist appointments?

JAMIE: Wha' dentist appointments?

DOREEN: Oh my god.

JAMIE: Look Dodi—(*Looking right.*) d'ere's a whale right over d'ere.

DOREEN: I could taste it that first night you showed up at my tent.

JAMIE: Yuh, had a little buzz on, hey b'y.

DOREEN: Didn't stop me, I guess. (*Looking right.*) Holy crap! It is a whale!

Throughout the next exchange, we hear that whale and others blowing water out of their blowholes.

JAMIE: Uh pothead.

DOREEN: A what?

JAMIE: Pot (*Rubbing his.*) head.

DOREEN: Oh right. I think the rest of the world calls them pilot whales.

JAMIE: Dur potheads. Like yer cousin Wally.

DOREEN: Jamie—

JAMIE: And uh bunch of he's buddies are d'ere too, luh—

DOREEN: I don't know what we're doing when you have to drink to—(*Looking right.*) LOOK AT ALL OF THEM!!

Sounds of whales blowing water into the air play successively.

JAMIE: D'ey ain't capelin, d'at's fur sure.

DOREEN: There must be ten of them!

JAMIE: Usually d'ey're in groups uh twenty to uh 'undred d'is time uh year. Every single one sprayin' friggin' snots deh size uh St. Pierre an' Miquelon.

DOREEN: A hundred? Are you serious?

JAMIE: Yes, me ducky.

DOREEN: Maybe we should head back.

JAMIE: What's deh trouble?

The sound of a large and very nearby blow. Perhaps a few more follow.

DOREEN: (*Shrieking, pointing to the left side of the dory.*) There's one right by the boat!

JAMIE: And one over 'ere, too, luh.

DOREEN: Ohmygod! Ohmygod!

JAMIE: Prob'ly a few under us, I'd say.

DOREEN: Jamie, do something!

By this time it should sound like approximately fifty pilot whales are swimming in and around the boat. JAMIE looks around, considering possible actions but he's generally not bothered. DOREEN puts her head in her lap, hoping for it all to be over. She looks up: JAMIE is cracking a beer.

JAMIE! WHAT THE FUCK??

JAMIE: D'ere yuh goes, swearin' again.

DOREEN: DO SOMETHING, YOU IDIOT!

JAMIE: D'ey're just passing t'rough.

DOREEN: IF YOU LOVE ME, YOU'LL DO—

The blow noises become more distant, and then leave altogether.

Something.

DOREEN breathes heavily, grabbing her chest and sprawling across her seat. JAMIE chugs his beer and opens another.

JAMIE: Canadian Light, Dodi?

DOREEN: I'm still courting this one. (*Opening hers.*) I'm sure beer is great for heart attacks. (*Swigging it.*) You know, I no longer feel as bad about those whale driving stories Uncle Art used to tell us.

JAMIE: "If yuh loves me, yuh'll do—"

DOREEN: Shut up.

JAMIE: (*Softly.*) "Something."

DOREEN: Shut up.

JAMIE: I must say…I misses yuh when I idn't 'ere, Dodi.

DOREEN: As much as when I was off the island?

JAMIE: Almost. 'Ard tuh compare tuh t'irteen years uh wond'rin' what deh bejesus 'appened to yuh, d'ough. (*Beat.*) It wadn't even fit. Deh first year yuh didn't come 'ome I punched away pretty much all deh gyprock in me basement. Fodder loved d'at.

DOREEN: Keep goin'. I like this confessional stuff.

JAMIE: Oh, well, 'ere's one fur yuh. (*Beat.*) Dodi, I didn't go on not one date till two er t'ree years afder high schoo.

DOREEN: For real?

JAMIE: Didn't see nobody. Nar one.

DOREEN raises an eyebrow, then laughs—not mean, but surprised.

No laughin' matter, missus. I was fucked right deh

fuck up. Not d'at I didn't 'ave no offers or nuddin'. Mind now. Bev asked me tuh ev'ry prom, ev'ry formal, ev'ry Norman's Cove/Long Cove weekend, ev'ry 'ockey game—fuck, she wanted me tuh go see 'er dermatologist wit'er one time.

DOREEN: When did you cave?

JAMIE: Funny story, act'chully. It was on Sep'tember deh elevent', two-thous'nd one.

DOREEN: You were inspired by terrorism?

JAMIE: No.

DOREEN: Firefighters?

JAMIE: No.

DOREEN: CNN?

JAMIE: No b'y. D'at jus' 'appened tuh be deh day I got fed up waitin' fur yuh, so I went over tuh Bev's place and told 'er, "Fuck it, I'll fuck yuh." So I did—in 'er fodder's shed. But d'en he caught us in deh middle uh deh act, just when him and he's two sons and me own fodder and all d'ey're friends wus bringin' in deh bull moose d'at d'ey'd jus' shot. D'ey cut deh fuckin' moose up in tuh quarters tuh fit it in deh back uh deh pickup, so when d'ey walks in d'ey're pourin' moose blood and innards all over deh floor—and d'ere's me and Bev naked on deh power saw. (*Beat.*) I put on me drawers and went straight 'ome. Turned on deh TV and I finds out d'at two towers crashed and t'ousands uh people is presumed dead. I t'ought I ruined deh world or somet'in'. Like I wadn't meant to uh done it a'tall.

DOREEN: Yet you've dated her ever since.

JAMIE: Yeah...but yuh frigged me up pretty good d'ere for a while.

DOREEN: For a while.

JAMIE: An' now. Yuh got me right fucked now.

DOREEN: You been talking to Uncle Art?

JAMIE: If I gets a few spare hours on me day off.

DOREEN: Recently?

JAMIE: Nah fur a week er so, no. Why?

DOREEN: Just wondering. (*Beat.*) Does he say anything about me?

JAMIE: Uh course.

DOREEN: Like what?

JAMIE: I dunno, girl. Lots uh t'ings I s'ppose.

DOREEN: Right.

JAMIE: Well, act'cually, he's mentioned uh few times—

DOREEN: What?

JAMIE: D'at yuh been actin' kinda strange when yuh goes tuh visit 'em. Quiet er somet'ing.

DOREEN: I find it hard, I guess.

JAMIE: I knows.

DOREEN: Plus his mind's going, Jamie.

JAMIE: Yes, I dare say. He 'asn't been no good for years, but he's riiiight gone now. I can't barely follow half uh what he says. Prob'ly 'avin' a bad time not gettin' he's share uh deh liquor too.

DOREEN: Yes.

JAMIE: What do yuh t'ink he'd t'ink about all d'is? Me and you?

DOREEN: I don't think he needs any abrupt news.

JAMIE: I means if he wus gonna know. What d'en?

DOREEN: I'm not sure what would happen, really.

JAMIE: Too bad dur was nudding yuh could do.

DOREEN: What do you mean?

JAMIE: To get 'em out.

DOREEN: Yeah, I wish.

JAMIE: Deh people at deh jail says he might be moved in deh next few weeks. To uh nuthouse or whatever.

DOREEN: That'd be better.

JAMIE: Prob'ly. (*Beat.*) Dodi, do yuh t'ink—

He stops himself.

DOREEN: Pardon?

JAMIE: Nudding. Look, let's nah get into all d'at. Deh past is nudding 'cause yuh can't do shit all about it. (*Beat.*) Guy Fawkes next week.

DOREEN: It is, isn't it?

JAMIE: And I t'inks I can get out 'ere fur it, if yuh wanna do somet'ing fur it.

DOREEN: What do you suggest?

JAMIE: Whattaya t'ink, girl? Our first Guy Fawkes Night in over uh decade...I figures we should go down Little Gut. Where we always went wit' Art'ur.

DOREEN: That would be great. (*Beat.*) Although we could try something different. Head over to Southern Cove Beach around dark.

JAMIE: Dodi...a lotta people goes tuh Sutter Cove Beach fur d'at bonfire.

DOREEN: So? (*Beat.*) So we'll just have to go to Little Gut.

JAMIE: We can still have are selves uh bonfire. I t'ought yuh would want to.

DOREEN: I definitely do. Now that I think of it, it's the only way to go.

JAMIE: Yeah, I t'inks it'll be good. And I wus t'inkin' I could drop by deh prison d'ere an' see if d'ey'd be so kind as tuh let deh poor feller come out 'ere wit' us fur a few days. Y'know, where he's goin' to uh mental 'ome anyways.

DOREEN: That won't work.

JAMIE: Wha'?

DOREEN: They won't go for it. He's just a delusional fire starter to them.

JAMIE: Might as well give'er a shot.

DOREEN: You never know how he might react.

JAMIE: He did fine seein' us 'round each udder fur years. I mean, we wouldn't be feelin' each udder up 'round 'em er nudding improper. He might be glad fur us. He never did like deh sight uh Bev.

DOREEN: I don't want to have to pretend for him. I'm already playing pretend for the entire town.

JAMIE: OK. I jus' t'ought it'd be good fur him tuh get out fur a bit, and tuh go tuh one he's fav'rite spots—

DOREEN: It's not very sensible.

JAMIE: C'mon Dodi. I feels fur 'em, b'y. He ain't got nobody, and—

DOREEN: He tried to kiss me, Jamie.

JAMIE: Wha'?

DOREEN: Twice.

JAMIE: When was d'is?

DOREEN: Before I left. And when I came back.

JAMIE: No he never.

DOREEN nods her head, looking rattled.

He did too. (*Beat.*) C'mon 'ere, girl. Come 'ere tuh me.

She complies. He wraps his arms around her. She cries.

DOREEN: My mom caught him the first time. He followed me home one night after I played Spotlight with you and some of the b'ys, and—

JAMIE: It's OK.

DOREEN: —and in the tent that first night I was back, he smothered me the whole time. Kept wanting me to kiss him. But I made him stop. I made him stop completely.

JAMIE: I'm sorry, Dodi. Yuh should uh told me.

DOREEN: I know. I'm sorry.

JAMIE: I understands. Yer fine. Yer wit' me now. (*Beat.*) D'at goddamn drunk won't never grow up.

DOREEN: I don't think he can. I don't think he'd even know what it would mean to try. (*Beat.*) But I do want to go to Little Gut with you. Now that— now that you know.

JAMIE: Yer on d'en. We're goin'.

DOREEN: Good. (*Beat.*) I can't believe you're here in front of me.

JAMIE: 'Ere we is. It ain't Big Tunnel, but ain't no shit hole nei'der.

DOREEN: The middle of the Atlantic does all right for itself.

JAMIE: FUCK!

DOREEN: What?

JAMIE: I forgot all about it—

JAMIE stands and retrieves a lifejacket from under his seat.

D'ere yuh are, me ducky.

JAMIE presents DOREEN with the lifejacket.

DOREEN: Aren't you supposed to put these on before the boat sets off?

JAMIE: Yuh, I gotta lay off deh beers a bit maybe.

DOREEN: Where's yours?

JAMIE: Don't got one.

DOREEN: You don't have a spare?

JAMIE: Don't keep none 'round usually. Bev never comes out.

DOREEN: (*Finding a tag.*) It's new.

JAMIE: Yuh.

DOREEN: You bought it for me?

JAMIE: Well yuh.

DOREEN: I miss you all the damn time, you know that?

JAMIE: No yuh don't!

DOREEN: I do!

JAMIE: Don't t'ink 'bout me a'tall, yuh fibber!

DOREEN: (*Laughing, sitting on his chest as they play.*) I MISSES YUH SOME BAD, B'Y!

JAMIE: Is d'at yur best Newfie?

DOREEN: No. (*Beat.*) I LOVES YUH TUH DEAT', MAH SON!

JAMIE: Dat wudn't bad. I bought a pack lunch too.

DOREEN: I really do love you.

JAMIE: I t'inks yer right cool too, b'y. So I brung chicken neck soup and uh bag uh weed—whattaya want first?

DOREEN: "I t'inks yer right cool…"

JAMIE: Only jokin', missus!

DOREEN: Good. 'Cause I was only joking about loving you.

JAMIE: Is d'at right—

DOREEN: What'd you actually bring?

JAMIE: I says I bought uh pack lunch—I didn't say uh t'ing 'bout sharin', hey b'y.

DOREEN: You're a twit—

JAMIE: An' yer uh twat—

DOREEN: EXCUSE ME.

JAMIE: I loves yuh, Dodi. Geeeeezus—get off me back, woman.

Scene 3

Monday at 4:00 PM. St. John's, Newfoundland. Lights up on ART, who's seemingly older and genuinely more distraught than before. He sits on a chair. DOREEN, dressed tidily and in bright autumn fabrics, enters and joins him at a meeting table.

DOREEN: Hello.

ART: What uh shock. Dodi Pretty.

DOREEN: Hi Uncle Art. I'm sorry it's been so long.

ART: If it idn't deh pretty Dodi Pretty!

DOREEN: Yes.

ART: You wus deh only Pretty d'at ever fit deh name.

DOREEN: I remember you saying so.

ART: It's true, girl—

DOREEN: Thanks.

ART: Take me older brudder, Tom-Pat, fur ezample.

DOREEN: I know.

ART: I seen flounders more good lookin' d'an d'at feller.

DOREEN: Yes.

ART: An' all me sisters 'ad 'air as coarse as toast. Well, yer mudder didn't, but she had d'at great big ten-story nose. Could uh been a tourist attraction if d'ere wus uh cafeteria up d'ere.

DOREEN: Uncle Art—

ART: Sorry. Yuh knows I didn't mean nudding by it. I loved yer mudder.

DOREEN: I know.

ART: Nah sure 'ow much she loved me back sometimes, mind yuh, but I felt some lot fur her deh whole time she wus alive.

DOREEN: Have a seat.

He does.

Are you OK?

ART: Bes' kind.

DOREEN: Really. How are you holding up?

ART: Fine, fine. Best kind, b'y.

DOREEN: Uncle Art, I know you're not fine. I know you don't like it here. You look shaken.

ART: I'm FINE, for fucksake. I told yuh d'at. (*Beat.*) I'm—I'm—I'm gonna go fix us some tea.

He goes to stand.

DOREEN: Uncle Art.

ART: (*Looking about the prison.*) Right, right. Outta tea.

ART's rambling was part sickness, part nervousness. Now he's quiet.

DOREEN: I'm sorry I haven't been more available. I'm trying to straighten out some job stuff. Career stuff maybe. Has Jamie been around?

ART rocks his head repeatedly. He licks his lips. He might move his lips as well, but no sound escapes from them.

Hello? (*Beat.*) So he hasn't been?

ART: I don't know wha's happenin' tuh d'at feller. Nah 'round as much as he wus.

DOREEN: I'm sure he's just very tied up with the business.

ART: Ain't been by in ages, Dodi. Jus' like you. Gives me bad feelin's.

DOREEN: Don't feel bad. Everything's best kind, remember? (Beat.) I hear they might be moving you soon. (*Beat.*) Uncle Art, I'm told they're going to move you to a new home. A better place than here. Is that true?

ART: Yuh, yuh. I'm taking off now deh once.

DOREEN: That's good. You'll do better there, I think.

ART: (*Now rocking a bit in his chair.*) Oh yuh.

DOREEN: Uncle Art.

ART: Yuh, yuh.

DOREEN: Uncle Art. Look at me.

ART: Yuh—

DOREEN: (*Whispering harshly.*) UNCLE ART.

ART's head darts up, his eyes locked on his niece.

Listen. They told me not to upset you. If I upset you, I have to leave. Do you understand?

ART: Yes.

DOREEN: Now I want to talk to you. I want to talk to you

about something. Something about our friend Jamie. OK? Is that going to upset you?

ART returns to rocking his body and nodding his head.

DOREEN: I don't want to upset you, but we have to talk about it.

ART rocks and bobs.

Uncle Art, I am seeing Jamie Griffiths. (*Beat.*) I love him. That can't be too leftfield, I don't think. You must have known. You must have sensed that before. (*Beat.*) But look, this is— this is the bad part. He— Uncle Art, he doesn't want me to see you anymore. He doesn't think it's good for me. (*Beat.*) I hope you comprehend that. I don't want to make you feel worse, but I also couldn't just stop coming in without—without seeing you. Saying bye. (*Beat.*) That's what I wanted you to know. I think you get it.

DOREEN stands and goes to leave.

ART: SIT—DOWN!

DOREEN: Don't raise your voice.

ART: SIT—DOWN!

DOREEN: OK. I'm sitting.

ART: Are yuh 'appy tuh be back?

DOREEN: I—what?

ART: Do yuh feel 'appy tuh be back 'ome?

DOREEN: Yes. I'm happy.

ART: Good. (*Beat.*)

DOREEN: I didn't mean for—I'm so sorry. (*Beat.*) Goodbye.

ART: WAIT!

DOREEN: I have to go.

ART: Why would yuh come back tuh me jus' tuh *get* back at me? Just tuh get rid uh me?

DOREEN: I didn't mean to.

ART: I can't take it in 'ere. Don't got me quad. Me tent. You. Don't got nudding 'ere.

DOREEN: It's OK.

ART: NO IT AIN'T! I'm sad in 'ere. I'm sad, Dodi. I'm sad 'cause you 'ATES me.

DOREEN: I don't hate you.

ART: Seems like it. (*Beat.*) I loves you. I'd do anyt'ing fur yuh.

ART rocks, nods and sobs.

DOREEN: I can't see you again. (*Beat.*) I brought you this.

DOREEN pushes a paper bag of takeout food across the table.

The guard said it was OK if you stayed here and ate it.

DOREEN starts to leave.

ART: I t'ought we wus all friends. I t'ought we loved each udder.

DOREEN hears this on her way but finishes the exit.

Yuh can't jus' walk out. I'm old now, Dodi! I miss it out d'ere. Miss deh wild blueberries. Miss deh rain beatin' down while I sleeps out in nowhere. (*Beat.*) We wus deh T'ree Blind Mice together. Boat uh ye's wus me mice. Yuh wus me friends.

ART tosses his bag of food to the floor.

Scene 4

Saturday at 2:37 PM. Little Gut, Chapel Arm. DOREEN and JAMIE have just come to the end of an ATV ride. It's all trees, water and bog for miles.

DOREEN: I thought you said we were following a "path."

JAMIE: Yuh, d'at was deh pat'.

DOREEN: Jamie, we were driving over small trees at one point.

JAMIE: Well…ain't much of uh ride if yuh idn't gettin' stuck.

DOREEN: You're a lunatic.

JAMIE: Mind now. (*Beat.*) Slut.

DOREEN: What'd you say to me?

JAMIE: I said…yuh best be putting up are tent er gettin' deh fire started.

DOREEN: Oh really.

JAMIE: Nah jokin', me ducky.

DOREEN: And what are you going to do?

JAMIE: I'm gonna 'ave uh smoke.

DOREEN: A smoke.

JAMIE: Needs a puff, b'y.

DOREEN: Got one for me?

JAMIE: You don't be at d'is stuff.

DOREEN: Well, not usually. But it is Guy Fawkes Night.

JAMIE: Get out've 'er.

DOREEN: I smoked during my undergrad.

JAMIE: Yer wha'?

DOREEN: Undergraduate. Degree. (*Beat.*) School.

JAMIE: Right.

DOREEN: It's an occasion! Come on.

JAMIE: (*Retrieving two cigarettes.*) 'Ere yuh go d'en.

DOREEN: Thank you.

DOREEN simply holds her cigarette for a time, feeling bad in a good way.

JAMIE: You'll pro'lly need one uh d'ese too.

JAMIE extends his hand with a lighter in it. He fires up DOREEN's cigarette and then his own.

DOREEN: Jerk.

JAMIE: Y'know…d'at's got ammonia in it.

DOREEN takes a puff. The harshness stings her lungs.

DOREEN: That sounds about right.

JAMIE: Yuh smokes like uh mainlander.

DOREEN: And you smoke like a Newfie. Which means all the time.

JAMIE: Is what I is, I says.

JAMIE grabs two beers out of his coat or a nearby bag/cooler. He's got his opened in seconds. DOREEN holds hers patiently.

DOREEN: I was thinking during the ride here—

JAMIE: Me too.

DOREEN: What were you thinking about?

JAMIE: Nah tellin'. What wus you t'inkin'?

DOREEN: Not telling.

JAMIE: Well fuck. Pointless, wha'?

DOREEN: Standstill.

JAMIE: Yer startin' tuh look a bit more comf'r'able wit' d'at cig'rette.

DOREEN: It's coming to me.

They smoke.

JAMIE: Dodi.

DOREEN: Yes?

JAMIE: What wus you t'inkin'?

DOREEN: You probably wouldn't want to hear it.

JAMIE: You wus t'inkin' about bein' on yer rag?

DOREEN: No. Fool.

JAMIE: Jus' guessin'. Bitch.

DOREEN: (*Laughing.*) Fine. I was just thinking...that you really shouldn't be drinking and driving. I mean, it's drinking and driving. There's a certain stigma there.

JAMIE: Not like it ain't been done before.

DOREEN: But then I thought, "So he's drinking. But look at him drive. He's still driving better than I could if I were sober."

JAMIE: Nah bad, wha'?

DOREEN: And that's what I thought over and over. Just how different we are. You can drink and drink and still do all of these things I think are difficult. Because it's second nature to you. I guess our natures contrast. Sometimes it just jumps on me.

JAMIE: Yer from 'ere too.

DOREEN: I know, but—

JAMIE: So what are yuh gettin' at?

DOREEN: I'm sorry I brought it up. I don't want to sully anything.

JAMIE: Sully, she says.

DOREEN: I'm sorry I used that word too. Bad word to use...at any time, really.

JAMIE: I don't mean tuh drink so much 'round yuh. I'm nah tanked er nudding. It just puts me in deh moment, I guess.

DOREEN: I want you to know that I'm...I'm going to buy a house.

JAMIE: Wha'?

DOREEN: I'm going to have a new home. I'm putting it right on my land. It's gonna be like the old one. A mini-home that I'll just build onto over the years as the money accumulates. I'll build it into a real house. (*Beat.*) And I've been looking into classes.

JAMIE: Wha' kind?

DOREEN: I want to get a trade. At first I thought of welding—Leslie-Anne just finished her courses and got a job straight away in Holyrood.

JAMIE: Can't barely smoke a cig'rette, but she t'inks 'er lungs can 'andle a lifetime uh welding chem'cals.

DOREEN: I thought of that too.

JAMIE: An'—?

DOREEN: (*Mumbling, with humor.*) I crossed welding off the list. So I had a few days with heat tracing in mind. Old Don Reid is on a rig off the coast of Africa six months of the year, and he says they're always looking for more people.

JAMIE: D'at idn't too glam'rous neider. And six mont's uh deh year..?

DOREEN: Precisely. So I quit thinking about that too. Mostly because I know what the perfect option is.

JAMIE: Oh yuh?

DOREEN: And so on Thursday I signed up for a nine-month program.

JAMIE: Nine mont's. (*Beat.*) Now *yer* pregnant!?

DOREEN: No. I'm taking classes in sprinkler installation.

JAMIE: Sprinklers?

DOREEN: Yep.

JAMIE: Yer full uh shit.

DOREEN: Nope. No shit. Sprinklers. Water.

JAMIE: I 'ad some women flirt wit' me before, but d'is is totally new.

DOREEN: In the meantime—

JAMIE: Wuh?

DOREEN: You might as well set up our tent.

JAMIE: Dodi—

DOREEN: What?

JAMIE: Yer somet'in else.

DOREEN: I dare say.

Scene 5

Friday at 6:10 P<. St. John's. A bright room in a mental health facility. ART, sitting on the floor, should wear clothes that are obviously different from his prison getup. He rubs his hands together in front of his chest as though there were a fire before him. He looks to his left, smiling, and then his right, smiling even wider. He inhales deeply.

ART: Nudding else on deh face uh d'is eart' like uh good bonfire, me little buddies. D'at cracklin' an' brightness still touches me just deh same as when I wus a youngster. We used tuh have all kinds uh fires—I'd make 'em wit' me brudders—in d'is very spot 'ere. D'ere's no finer spot d'an Little Gut Pond. No sir. It can be so cold yer skin gets right tight an' mad atcha just fur wearing it out in such conditions...an' d'en yuh sits in front of uh fire like d'is 'ere one. All d'at tension melts on away down to yer feet like ice cream yuh forgot tuh put in deh freezer, hey b'y. An' yer warm. An' yer nat'ral. Deh fire feels so good yuh just can't believe d'at Hell is blessed wit' uh gift like d'at. No sir. I knows I don't t'ink uh Hell like d'at...I t'inks it's just uh great big meat locker wit' no meat. It's all cold wit' no chunks uh wood for no bonfire. Know what I means? (*Beat.*) Jamie, mah son, get d'at stick outta duh fire. Yer marshmallow's blacker d'an deh nigger dentist d'ey got out in Whitbourne. Yes, yes. I knows yuh likes it burnt, but leave it in d'ere any longer an' all ye'll have left tuh eat is yer stick, yuh silly runt yuh. Luh—Dodi got it down pat. Her weenie's roasted tuh perfection, mah son. I can tell from here d'at yuh got d'at cooked right t'rough, me dear. Bang on job, ducky. Guy Fawkes heself couldn't uh took deh fire tuh d'at any better. Wha's d'at? Yuh don't know who Guy Fawkes is? Well, I told yuh jus' last year, Dodi. Ohhh yes b'y. Yuh forgets, do yuh? Oh yeees—you forgets too, eh Jamie? S'ppose I'll just have tuh waste more uh me breat' tellin' yuh again now. An' d'en again next year. You'll have me choked one day, hey b'y. What're you laughin' at d'ere, missy? All right, all right. I'll tell yuh. Guy Fawkes...was a man. Yuh, yuh. "No duh" ye says. Anyway—he was a man, a British man, a British Roman Cat'lic man, who took it upon heself tuh try and blow up deh 'Ouses uh Parliament way, way back when deh Protestants wus all fancy an' in charge. Oh, deh 'Ouses uh Parliament is in England, Jamie. No, not yet, Dodi—I'll get out deh sparklers in just a minute. Now lemme finish. See, Mr. Guy Fawkes was caught by d'em Anglicans. One Anglican who would uh been dead if deh Gunpowder Plot had gone t'rough—man by deh name uh 'Andwood... er wus it 'Eywood...well, Somet'ingwood. He took deh torch d'at would uh changed 'istory right outta Fawkes' 'ands. So deh bad guys wanted tuh kill Fawkes right slow—really make deh bugger suffer, like. D'ey wanted 'em 'anged, drawn out and cut in tuh quarters. He was doomed, b'ys. But get uh load uh d'is now: d'at shifty son of uh bitch—s'cuse me French—he got outta deh worst uh it, man. He jumped from deh platform d'ey was gonna 'ang 'em from and broke he's neck right off deh bat. Saved heself a whole lotta torture, tell yuh d'at. I t'inks d'at makes bonfires like d'is smell all deh nicer. Jus' knowin' he got caught doin' somet'in' he believed in, but still wadn't about to give no one no extra satisfaction. I can smell a real believer in every bonfire I ever been to. He wus a real fighter, I t'inks. What do ye's t'ink? (*Beat.*) Wuh's d'is now! Both uh ye's past out. Yer bedtimes long gone, yuh little darlings. I loves boat uh ye's. Ye'll never know how much. D'at Mr. Fawkes was a fighter, man.

ART is lost in the fictitious flames in front of him.

Yer lookin' right fit, Jamie. Must be all d'at ball yuh plays on deh garden. Even when yer sleepin', yer arse looks tight.

ART reaches for a fictional backside, lightly pulling his finger across it. There's guilt in the movement.

I loves d'is place. I loves when you falls asleep wit' yer face right on me lap, Dodi. Yer mout's some warm.Yer such perfect kids. Perfect angels.

Scene 6

Sunday at 12:14 PM. Chapel Arm. A dank basement with unnecessary rugs that are even more unnecessarily filthy. An elderly couch of stains, rips, creases and faded flowers mopes in front of a generously nicked bar. The bar, rarely touched by genuinely functional adults, has some fearsome poker hands taped to it, as well as a lady poster or two from the informative pages of Maxim. *An old hunting license might be on display, but certainly there's a potrait of a limp bull moose. There's probably a broken Big Mouth Billy Bass loitering at the bar. DOREEN, a 29-year-old sprinkler student, lies on the couch, thankfully separated from its withered skin by a quilt in slightly better condition; she attentively scans a binder filled with laminated notes. She's humming. Then singing. She isn't belting—it's just a favourite song to help the studying bounce along.*

DOREEN: We are children, children of the light. We are shining, in the darkness of the night, hope for this world. Joy through all the land, touch the heart of everyone, take everybody's—

JAMIE enters with a tray that holds two cups of coffee and two plates of breakfast.

JAMIE: You still knows deh words.

DOREEN: (*Slightly embarrassed.*) I didn't know you were listening.

JAMIE: Yer singin's gotten uh little better since you wus uh kid.

DOREEN: Who are you this morning—Roy Orbison?

JAMIE: Who? (*Beat.*) Weird d'at uh churchy song like d'at would stay with yuh so long, hey?

DOREEN: It was a nice song. Sort of heartening. That said, it's funny you still like it given the amount of time you spend listening to OZ FM.

JAMIE: I'd take "Children uh deh Light" over Zeppelin er Petty any day.

DOREEN: Sex, drugs and Catholic hymns.

JAMIE: Don't you worry 'bout music. You worry 'bout eatin' every spec uh grease on d'at plate. D'at's me one of uh kind breakfast right d'ere.

DOREEN: Just as long as you don't listen to Nickelback, I guess.

DOREEN laughs. JAMIE avoids eye contact.

Oh Jesus, you do.

JAMIE: Well, nah lately, hey.

DOREEN: That's reprehensible, Jamie.

JAMIE: I mostly listens to d'ey're old stuff.

DOREEN: Why?

JAMIE: I dunno.

DOREEN: They're the band even really bad people make fun of.

JAMIE: D'ey do? I just likes deh song 'bout beating up women.

DOREEN: Fair enough.

JAMIE: Nah 'cause I don't like women—it just sounds rocky, like.

DOREEN: This is good breakfast.

JAMIE: I don't like Nickelback no more, OK?

DOREEN: OK. (*Beat.*) Wow. The hash browns are particularly well done.

JAMIE: Dur burnt?

DOREEN: No. Well done…like, good job.

JAMIE: Oh. T'anks. (*Beat.*) I don't even own none uh d'ey're albums, y'know.

DOREEN: Jamie. I don't care what you listen to. And really. Thanks for making me breakfast.

JAMIE: Welcome, me dear. (*Beat.*) Made it meself. Yuh know, yuh shouldn't be pickin' on me. Yuh checked out deh bar today?

DOREEN: What's this about?

JAMIE: Go over yuh has a peek.

DOREEN finishes chewing and walks to the bar. She fidgets with things, investigating.

DOREEN: There's nothing.

JAMIE: You got 'er, Pontiac.

DOREEN: So—

JAMIE: I cleared it all out.

DOREEN: No beer?

JAMIE: Nar one.

DOREEN: You even got rid of that really old Scotch.

JAMIE: Sold it to uh few grade niners outside deh Esso.

DOREEN: Jamie!

JAMIE: Just foolin', b'y.

DOREEN: (*Returning to her plate.*) I'm glad.

JAMIE: Me too.

DOREEN: Do you want some of my bacon?

JAMIE: (*Immediately offended.*) I t'ought yuh said it was ex'llent.

DOREEN: It is excellent.

JAMIE: D'en eat wha's on yer plate.

DOREEN: I just don't eat much meat.

JAMIE: Why nah?

DOREEN: I don't know.

JAMIE: Lard fuck.

DOREEN: It's not like I don't eat meat. I just—here, take some bacon.

JAMIE: Give 'er here. I likes me meat. (*Beat.*) How're deh studies goin'?

DOREEN: Not bad at all.

JAMIE: Ye'll pass no problem.

DOREEN: I hope so.

JAMIE: Now I just needs tuh figure out 'ow tuh tell me fodder tuh hire on uh woman.

DOREEN: Indeed.

JAMIE: Let alone deh woman I kinda been sleepin' wit' lately.

DOREEN: "Say, you ought to hire this great childhood friend I've been committing adultery with. She's really cute, huh?"

JAMIE: Yer really stayin' d'is time, ain't yuh?

DOREEN: Yuh-huh.

JAMIE: For real now.

DOREEN: I'm staying. In my new house when it's ready.

JAMIE: Good girl.

DOREEN: But I mean…I'm no carpenter.

JAMIE: No shit.

DOREEN: Not to—

JAMIE: I wants to. I'm goin' to.

DOREEN: I'm thinking hardwood floors.

JAMIE: I was gonna say—

They kiss. They giggle. This continues with periodic lifts in energy for several moments. Meanwhile, BEV appears at the edge of the stage, heartsick. She stands behind the door for a time with a black purse in hand. She takes a breath, slides her key into the door to JAMIE's basement, and enters almost instantly, like she's known the movement personally. When she walks in, nothing happens that one could describe as "bursting" or "popping" or even "abrupt." It's agonizingly slow. JAMIE gingerly relinquishes his mount on DOREEN. He stands, holding his upper arms in his trembling hands out of some coldness and much uneasiness. DOREEN stands slightly behind him, not quite staring ahead at BEV. BEV is stoic.

BEV: Hey b'ys.

JAMIE: Bev.

BEV: D'is idn't really news tuh me, Jamie.

JAMIE: OK.

BEV: I knew it wus gonna 'appen. I knew when she—I knew. And I knows yuh lied tuh me, Jamie. I knows you wus full uh shit. I never said nudding 'cause I never wanted tuh know fur sure—officially, like. Whatever you two got—

JAMIE: Can we—

BEV: I knew when she was right 'ere. Standin' right here. When you wus standing 'ere, Dodi, in d'is spot. I knew yuh wus gonna get 'im.

DOREEN: I'm sorry, Bev.

JAMIE: Bev—

BEV: I knew d'en, and I known when I seen ye's at yer locker in school—

JAMIE: We needs—

BEV: And I knew all deh way back tuh when ye's told Mrs. Baron yuh wanted yer cubbyholes next to each udder in grade kindergarten.

JAMIE: Look, we needs tuh 'ave a long talk—

BEV: We needs tuh talk. But it don't need tuh be long.

JAMIE: Whattaya mean?

BEV: My message is right simple.

JAMIE: D'is idn't simple no more—

BEV: Shut up! Stop contradictin' everyt'in' I says. You guys don't get tuh push me out no more! D'is idn't grade five no more—stop bein' so 'igh an' mighty an' mis'r'ble. If yuh wants each udder so bad, stop findin' hidin' spots. Stop yer lyin'. Stop treatin' me like uh retard yuh keeps around but don't want tuh spend no real time wit'.

DOREEN: Bev, we didn't mean—

BEV: Fuck you. (*Staring at JAMIE.*) Fuck her, Jamie. I 'ates her. And you knew d'at.

JAMIE: D'is is bad, Bev. I knows it is.

BEV: Yer shit, Jamie.

JAMIE: I'm sorry.

BEV: Ye boat ain't wort' shit.

JAMIE: I'm sorry.

BEV: Stop sayin' d'at. I don't need d'at. You two's t'ing yuh got goin' on—d'at ye's 'ad going on since day one—it may uh left me wit'out uh 'usband. Wit'out a real boyfriend, hey b'y. And yer little affair might uh even been more important d'an yer first born, Jamie. But it idn't gonna kill me. An' it idn't gonna kill Little James. At least we're d'at lucky.

JAMIE: I never meant to hurt ye's.

BEV: I'd believe d'at if yuh wus a stranger, Jamie. But yuh knew— yuh had to uh known you wus gonna hurt us eventually. Yuh just kept puttin' off when, didn't yuh?

JAMIE: Yes.

BEV: Why am I so borin' tuh yuh? It don't matter no more, but I still wants tuh know.

JAMIE: You're a great woman, Bev.

BEV: Great woman yuh never followed after like yuh does her. When you t'ink you'll get borin', Dodi?

JAMIE: Yuh didn't deserve d'is, Bev. Uh course yuh never.

BEV: Neid'er did Art. How can yuh even look at each udder knowin' what ye's did tuh him?

JAMIE: Wha'?

BEV: Art'er.

DOREEN: Did something happen?

BEV: Y'knows, right?

JAMIE: Knows wha', Bev?

BEV: Ye's really don't know, do yuh's?

DOREEN: What's going on?

JAMIE: C'mon, Bev.

BEV: You lovebirds've been in uh nest so far up yuh couldn't even see yer friend wus rottin' away. Yer sick'ning, b'ys. Yah makes me sick. I 'ope someday yeh realizes 'ow fucked up d'is makes ye's.

DOREEN: Tell us, Bev!

BEV: He's dead. (*Beat.*)

JAMIE: He can't be, b'y. He jus' got moved.

DOREEN: You're lyin'.

BEV: No.

JAMIE: Who told you?

BEV: Yer mudder called me from deh junction.

DOREEN: Please say he's OK, Bev.

BEV: No, he's fuckin' not. He's dead.

JAMIE: Oh mah god.

DOREEN: I know you're upset, Bev, but—

BEV: S'got nudding tuh do wit' me bein' upset. I am very upset. I am low as shit tuh boat uh ye's but d'at didn't kill Art'ur. He idn't gone because I feels like shit. He's dead because he felt even lower d'an me—like more of uh outsider d'an I does. He only 'ad two friends left in deh world and look who d'ey wus. Two liars who can't get enough uh each udder's bullshit.

JAMIE: Lord fuck, Art'er…

DOREEN: You better be telling the truth.

BEV: Look at me, yuh liar. Do I look like a liar, Dodi? Do I look like *you*? No, I don't. Maybe d'at's half uh what d'is wus about anyways.

DOREEN: No!

JAMIE: Wha' happened? Wha'—

BEV: He hung he's self in uh bat'room. Tied he's shirt around he's t'roat—

DOREEN: Stop.

BEV: 'Ung he's self from a stall.

DOREEN: Please! I can't—

BEV: Yer mudder says he's shirt gave out and he 'it he's 'ead. Pro'lly died pretty quick if d'at 'elps, but I don't really care too much if it do, tuh be honest.

JAMIE: Shut the fuck up, Bev.

A momentary hush.

It's 'er uncle, b'y.

BEV: *(To DOREEN.)* Sorry fur yer loss. (*To JAMIE.*) Sorry for all yer losses too, Jamie.

BEV pulls a pack of Canadian Classics cigarettes out of her purse and tosses it at JAMIE.

I quit, remember.

She exits in a hurry. DOREEN and JAMIE are left staring at each other.

The End.